BEST DRESSED

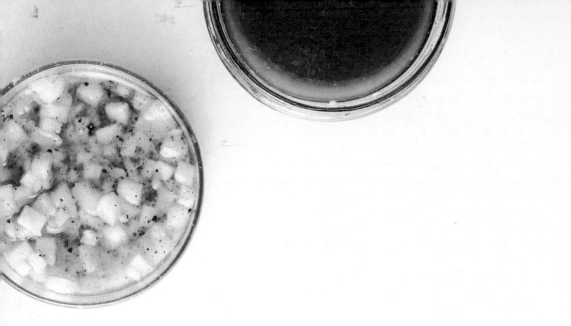

BEST DRESSED

50 Recipes, Endless Salad Inspiration

Dawn Yanagihara & Adam Ried

Photographs by Nicole Franzen

CHRONICLE BOOKS
SAN FRANCISCO

Library of Congress Cataloging-in-Publication Data:

Names: Yanagihara, Dawn, author. | Ried, Adam, author.
Title: Best dressed : 50 recipes, endless salad inspiration /
by Dawn Yanagihara and Adam Ried.
Description: San Francisco, CA : Chronicle Books, [2016] | Includes index.
Identifiers: LCCN 2015049121 | ISBN 9781452155142 (hardcover : alk. paper)
Subjects: LCSH: Salad dressing. | LCGFT: Cookbooks.
Classification: LCC TX819.S27 Y36 2016 | DDC 641.81/4—dc23 LC record
available at https://lccn.loc.gov/2015049121

Manufactured in China

Designed by Alice Chau

Photographs by Nicole Franzen
Food styling by Erin Quon
Prop styling by Kira Corbin

Chronicle books and gifts are available at special quantity discounts to corporations, professional associations, literacy programs, and other organizations. For details and discount information, please contact our premiums department at corporatesales@chroniclebooks.com or at 1-800-759-0190.

10 9 8 7 6 5 4 3 2 1

Chronicle Books LLC
680 Second Street
San Francisco, California 94107
www.chroniclebooks.com

ACKNOWLEDGMENTS

FROM DAWN

For creating such a beaut of a cookbook, I'd like to thank the terrific and wonderfully talented team at Chronicle Books—Sarah Billingsley, Deanne Katz, Alice Chau, Doug Ogan, Sara Golski, Tera Killip, Ellen Wheat, and Steve Kim. Sarah was our editor extraordinaire, and to her I owe a huge debt of gratitude for the opportunity to write this book. Nicole Franzen, Erin Quon, and Kira Corbin brought the recipes to life and made humble dressings and salads look stunning.

Adam Ried is the best coauthor one could ask for, and I consider myself fortunate to have had the chance to collaborate with him. Sandra Wu is a recipe-testing pro on whom I count every time—a big thank-you goes out to her. Last, but certainly not least, I'd like to thank my mom, Barbara Yanagihara, and my better half, Christyan Mitchell, for all their support throughout the years.

FROM ADAM

You could say that my part in this book results from doctor's orders. A few years back I wrote a book on milkshakes, which, over the course of a summer, occasioned the consumption of . . . ahem . . . a lot of milkshakes. In the fall, I had my annual physical, including blood tests for cholesterol and triglycerides and such. With the results in hand, my doctor, Ricardo Wellisch, looked me straight in the eye and said, "Now how about a book on lettuce and lemon juice?" While you won't find plain lettuce and lemon juice in this book, it's still a big step in the right direction. Here's to you, Dr. Wellisch!

A monster thanks, of course, to Dawn—friend, palate, opportunity maker, and co-conspirator par excellence. Thanks also to Sandra Wu for spot-on recipe testing and all-around loveliness, to my sister Amanda Hewell and my brother Josh Ried for their love and support, and our rockin' Chronicle team—editor Sarah Billingsley, Deanne Katz, managing editors Doug Ogan and Sara Golski, designer Alice Chau, Ellen Wheat, Tera Killip, Steve Kim, Nicole Franzen, Erin Quon, and Kira Corbin—for bringing the book to life with style and care.

CONTENTS

RICH

TOPPINGS

INTRODUCTION

Any enthusiastic eater, backyard gardener, or vegetable farmer will tell you that lettuces and greens have their own flavors and personalities. Indeed they do, and fresh, flavorful produce is important for making any salad good. But we all know it's the dressing that makes the salad. From a simple bowlful of lettuce to an elaborate combination of greens with cooked veggies, proteins, grains, and cheese, it's the dressing that pulls it all together, defining a salad's character, sending it in one ethnic direction or another (or none), and complementing other ingredients so they can do their best work on your palate.

Dressing a salad often intimidates a cook—even our food-obsessed friends are quick to hand off the job to a willing kitchen helper. Whether you've been the cook or the helper, you'll find this book to be a handy little volume. In it is a range of vinaigrettes and dressings, from traditional to modern, to help you indulge every salad-y whim. Looking for a buttoned-down, quiet, classic French vinaigrette to dress a simple green salad? We can do that. Need something with a touch more depth and mystery? How about a suave Pinot Noir or citrus, honey, and rosemary vinaigrette? Craving something rich? Look into our browned butter vinaigrette or toasted sesame dressing. There are dressings here to create salads for any mood.

Though some dressings in the book will strike familiar chords—ranch, blue cheese, Caesar—we modernize the old formulas a bit and create all new dressings with fresh, pure flavors and wholesome ingredients. We ditch heavy mayonnaise and sour cream and find creaminess in nuts and

nut butters, tahini, and even bread. Moreover, we take full advantage of the array of international ingredients in today's well-stocked grocery stores, from pomegranate molasses to miso to chia seeds. Combined with care and imagination, ingredients once exotic but now within easy reach can launch even a run-of-the-mill salad in exciting directions.

The dressing recipes are organized into three chapters: Bright, Bold, and Rich. Bright dressings are ones that sparkle with high notes; have fresh, vibrant flavors; or lean heavily on acidity for character. Bold dressings are high-impact, pack a lot of flavor into a small space, and are big-time attention-getters. Rich dressings are just as they sound—supple and sumptuous.

Since not every dressing matches with every type of salad green (for example, ranch dressing would crush delicate mesclun), each dressing recipe offers basic "Serve on" suggestions for building your salad—items such as greens, roasted vegetables, and fruits. Beyond that, we offer ideas for "Extras"—additions to make the salad more complete and garnishes to make it sublime. But keep in mind that our suggestions just scratch the surface, and there are delicious salads out there just waiting to be created.

The fourth chapter covers the last items to go onto a salad: Toppings. Think toasty, nutty, savory granola and crisp, irresistible fried shallots. Although garnishes such as these might be considered superfluous, a sprinkle of this or a scattering of that can elevate a salad from workaday to wonderful.

INGREDIENTS

It's been said before: great results depend as much on good ingredients as on solid recipes. With salad dressings, this is especially true, since the ingredients are few. So it stands to reason that the better and more carefully chosen the ingredients are, the more delicious your salads will be.

In this section, we'll describe the basic components of most salad dressings—oils, acids, and flavorings (discussed in descending order of amount used)—and explain the types that are commonly used in these recipes.

OILS

Without oil, there are no vinaigrettes—in fact, there would be precious few dressings. Oil carries flavor, adds luster, and helps a dressing cling to a salad.

Oil doesn't stay fresh forever. Light, heat, and air are the enemies of freshness, so keep oils well sealed and stored in a dark, relatively cool spot. And, just as you do with milk or cream before using it, give your oil a quick sniff before pouring it to ensure that no rancid or off odors or flavors have developed.

NEUTRAL OILS

Neutral oils have little to no detectable fragrance or flavor (and higher smoke points than olive oil). Many types of oil fit into this category, including canola, vegetable, corn, sunflower, safflower, grapeseed, and some would say peanut (though we're not convinced about that—we swear that sometimes you can taste it). In recipes that call for neutral oil, we specify canola because it's so common you probably have a bottle in your kitchen, as well as sunflower and safflower, which, to us, have an especially clean flavor.

So, in vinaigrettes and dressings with few ingredients, where the flavor of each one really counts, why are we talking about oils without any flavor? Because with some dressings, the flavor of olive oil just doesn't work. A flavorless oil will give the dressing the volume and consistency it needs without obscuring or conflicting with other flavors.

NUT OILS

Oils pressed from nuts—think walnuts, hazelnuts, or almonds—range in flavor from mild to robust. Raw nut oils are light in color and flavor, whereas their toasted/roasted versions are darker, highly aromatic, and more forceful.

While we love toasted nut oils, their flavors can dominate a dressing and throw the balance out of whack. So in some recipes, such as in Pomegranate Molasses–Walnut Oil Vinaigrette (page 54) or Maple-Mustard Vinaigrette (page 49), you'll find that we also use another oil to keep the nut oil in check.

All nut oils are more perishable than olive oil and neutral oils, so keep them in the refrigerator. Cold temperatures cause some types of oil to congeal; if yours has, let it stand at room temperature for 20 to 30 minutes, until it's fluid enough to pour.

OLIVE OIL

The most flavorful type of olive oil, and what we specify most often, is extra-virgin. Olives are "pressed" (or spun in a centrifuge) for oil several times, and extra-virgin is obtained from the first pressing, without the use of heat or chemicals. Extra-virgin's acidity level is no greater than 1 percent, which accounts in large part for its distinct yet relatively mellow flavor.

Extra-virgin olive oils offer a wide range of fragrance and flavor notes, including fruity, buttery, herbaceous, grassy, and peppery. These characteristics stand out more in costly artisanal oils; if you have one of these, save it for use as a finishing oil. A flavorful extra-virgin olive oil from the supermarket is fine for salad dressings.

You'll see that in some recipes, such as Apple Cider, Grainy Mustard, and Shallot Vinaigrette (page 26) and Fresh Mint Vinaigrette (page 30), we specify a mild-tasting extra-virgin olive oil. If your olive oil is assertive, mix it with an equal quantity of neutral oil (see page 10) to temper its flavor.

As olive oil classifications descend to "virgin" and then "pure" or "olive oil," so do flavor nuances. In supermarkets, you'll also encounter "light" olive oil, which is aggressively filtered to be lighter still in color, fragrance, and flavor. Though some might disagree, we consider light olive oil a neutral oil.

SESAME OIL

Sesame oil can be pressed from either raw or toasted sesame seeds. Raw sesame oil is light in color and relatively mild in taste. Toasted sesame oil, on the other hand, resembles dark maple syrup in color; has a rich, heady aroma; and is intense and assertive in flavor. Toasted sesame oil is the type you'll find in a few recipes (of the Asian ilk) in this book. Just a little toasted sesame oil goes a long way, so it's used only in very small amounts as a flavor accent. Like nut oils, sesame oil, both raw and toasted, should be stored in the refrigerator to extend its shelf life.

ACIDS

Vinaigrettes and dressings require some type of acidic ingredient for flavor, brightness, and balance. Here's a quick rundown of the acids we rely on most.

APPLE CIDER VINEGAR

To point out the obvious, apple cider vinegar is made from fermented apple juice, which gives it both bold fruitiness and an earthy quality. We prefer the flavor and aroma of raw unfiltered apple cider vinegar.

LEMON AND LIME JUICE

Freshly squeezed, please. Bottled? Don't bother. Bottled citrus juices taste harsh compared to the real deal. When shopping for both lemons and limes, look for fruit that's plump and round, has smoothish skin, yields slightly when you squeeze it gently, and feels heavy for its size. To get the most juice from a lemon or lime, we roll it back and forth on the work surface using light pressure before cutting it.

RICE VINEGAR

Delicate, mild, and ever so slightly sweet, rice vinegar is a great match for ingredients with subtle flavors and in Asian-inspired dressings. When shopping, avoid seasoned rice vinegar, which contains salt and sugar.

SHERRY VINEGAR

Made from the wine of the same name, sherry vinegar is our MVP for its subtle sweetness, nutty and woodsy notes, richness, and adaptability. Distinct and flavorful, sherry vinegar holds its own with other assertive ingredients. It's common to see the term *vinagre de Jerez* on the label; Jerez is the famous sherry-producing region of Spain.

WHITE BALSAMIC VINEGAR

You may notice the absence of regular balsamic vinegar in these recipes. While we love inky, syrupy balsamic vinegar as a condiment, we're not mad for its color in vinaigrettes and dressings because it can make for dark and murky mixtures.

Enter white balsamic vinegar. Whereas regular balsamic vinegar is caramelized in both flavor and color, and aged in charred wood barrels that darken it further, white balsamic is produced at lower temperatures under pressure and aged in uncharred barrels to limit darkening. White balsamic has some of the sweetness of its dark sibling, but it's less syrupy and arguably less complex. We see that as a positive, though. To us, white balsamic tastes lighter and cleaner, and we feel it makes a more handsome vinaigrette.

WINE VINEGAR, RED AND WHITE

Wine vinegars are the John Q. Public of the vinegar world—commonplace and somewhat anonymous. In salad dressings, we choose wine vinegars when we're looking for a nondescript brightness—one without distinct flavor traits. In our experience, red wine vinegars tend toward sharp; white wine vinegars are smoother, making them, generally speaking, our preference.

FLAVORINGS

Oils and acids are just part of the story; full flavor depends on a few other ingredients.

GARLIC

We would argue that fresh garlic is as essential to life as water and air. When choosing garlic, look for heads that are plump, tight, and firm when squeezed in your palm.

As garlic ages, a pale green germ will develop in the center of each clove. We notice a hot, bitter flavor in the germ, so we remove it. Simply halve the clove lengthwise, look for a green core in each half, and, if present, pry it out with the tip of the knife. (A very young germ may be yellowish and not as sharp in flavor, but remove it anyway since you've cut open the clove.)

To keep salad eaters from biting into pieces of raw garlic, we often call for cloves to be grated or minced to a paste. Grating is the speedier method and is best done on a rasp-style grater (such as a Microplane). To mince to a paste, first chop the garlic, sprinkle with a pinch of kosher salt, and continue to chop, occasionally pressing and grinding with the flat of the knife blade, until the garlic is quite smooth.

HERBS

When it comes to herbs in salad dressings, we apply the same logic that we do to lemon juice: Stick with fresh. Some dried herbs have their place, namely in stews, braises, and soups, but we dislike them in salad dressing. The price you pay for the potent flavor of fresh herbs is that they're highly perishable. We try to buy the smallest quantities we can find (hint: sometimes we look for small amounts of several herbs packaged together in poultry or seafood blends) and replace them as needed.

KOSHER SALT

Of the many types of salt available these days, for dressings we prefer kosher salt for its clean flavor, grab-ably large crystals, and dissolvability. Diamond Crystal and Morton's are the two most widely available brands, and their crystal sizes differ. Morton's has a larger, flatter flake that compacts more and therefore weighs more per volume measurement. We use Diamond Crystal, and all the recipes in this book were developed with it. We suggest that you use it too, if possible. If you need to use Morton's, start by using about 30 percent less than the recipe specifies; if the dressing doesn't taste right, add a little more.

Iodized table salt tastes a little funky to us, but it's not a disaster flavorwise. If table salt is what you have, use it, but use about 50 percent less than you would kosher salt.

MUSTARD

Mustard is a dressing multitasker. Depending on the quantity added, it can be a subtle flavor enhancer, a mild flavor element, or a bold flavor force. And it's always an aid to emulsification, contributing to the smooth consistency that is a goal of most dressing recipes. We often use Dijon mustard for its sophisticated, winey notes and smooth consistency, but we reach for whole-grain mustard when we're looking to add a little texture and visual interest to a dressing.

PEPPER, BLACK AND WHITE

Black pepper—freshly ground, please. Enough said.

White peppercorns are black peppercorns with their hulls removed. Their flavor is milder and sweeter than that of black pepper, and is a good match for many Asian-accented foods. Black pepper can stand in for white pepper, if that's what you have—just use less of it.

SHALLOTS

We use shallots to flavor a lot of these dressings because they provide an oniony pungency (shallots and onions are both in the Allium family) that's noticeably less brash than that of their larger cousins.

Shop for shallots that appear plump and are firm, without a spongy feel, shriveled ends, or obvious sprouts. Like onions and garlic, keep shallots somewhere dry, cool, and well ventilated, but not in the refrigerator.

GREENS WE KNOW AND LOVE

Arugula is tart and peppery, and depending on the type, it can be downright sharp. The texture is delicate, so the leaves are quick to wilt. We're partial to baby arugula rather than mature arugula.

Baby kale has a flavor not unlike that of baby spinach, and a sturdier texture.

Baby spinach has a slightly tangy, mineral-rich flavor and texture between delicate and sturdy. We opt for baby spinach rather than the dense, crinkly leaves of mature bunch spinach.

Butter/Bibb lettuce has a mild, sweet flavor and relatively delicate texture. Boston lettuce is a type of butter lettuce.

Cabbage is mild and sweet. Its crunchy, super-sturdy texture means it should be shredded finely. It also takes well to braising, sautéing, and stir-frying.

Endive has a very mild bitterness and small, succulent, oblong leaves with sturdy cores and delicate edges.

Escarole is another great salad green with a mildly bitter flavor. The stems are crisp and sturdy, and the leaves are quite frilly.

Flat-leaf parsley is generally thought of as an herb, but its deep green, tender leaves make a perfect counterpoint to a wide range of greens, from sweet to bitter. Parsley's flavor is mild but mineral and grassy.

Frisée has a distinctly and pleasantly bitter flavor and lacy leaves that can be bogged down by thick dressings.

Green leaf lettuce has a mild, sweet flavor and a texture at the midpoint of delicate and sturdy.

Iceberg lettuce is often overlooked or even maligned. It has its place—under Avocado Ranch, Sweet and Spicy Peanut, and Buttermilk Black-and-Blue dressings.

Lacinato kale has a deeply mineral, earthy flavor and a very sturdy texture that softens and becomes more pleasing when rubbed with dressing and allowed to rest for about 30 minutes.

Mesclun is a colorful mix of baby lettuces with a range of generally mild flavors and very delicate, easily overwhelmed textures.

Mizuna is a Japanese green that is becoming more widely available. The slender, serrated leaves have a slightly peppery bite but are not quite as assertive as arugula.

Radicchio has gorgeous white-and-claret-colored leaves, with a mildly peppery flavor and, like endive, sturdy cores and tender edges. Cut into wedges, heads of radicchio take well to a brief visit on a hot grill.

Red leaf lettuce has a mild, sweet flavor and a texture more delicate than most green leaf varieties, but sturdier than really delicate greens like mesclun.

Romaine is one of our often-chosen salad greens. It has a mild, sweet flavor and a sturdy, ready-for-almost-every-type-of-dressing texture. Halved romaine hearts are great when charred on a hot grill.

Watercress has a bold, spicy, peppery flavor. The leaves are delicate and stems are abundant. We're fans of "live" watercress, which is sold with roots attached, because the leaves contain much less grit and the stems are tender.

EQUIPMENT

To prepare many of the recipes in this book, the only pieces of equipment you'll need are a knife, cutting board, measuring spoons and cups, and a bowl for tossing the salad—they're all probably in your kitchen right now. Still, a couple of other items will be very useful.

GLASS JARS

We are proponents of using a glass jar to mix a vinaigrette (you'll read more about this in Techniques, page 20). Special jars aren't needed—just clean glass ones with secure-fitting lids and 1- to 1½-cup [240- to 360-ml] capacities. An empty salsa or jam jar fits the bill nicely. If you'll be putting hot liquid into the jar (a couple of our recipes have you doing so), make sure that the jar is heatproof and sturdy.

IMMERSION BLENDER

For recipes that require blending, we recommend using an immersion blender, a.k.a. a stick blender. This tool, often used for making soup, is also talented at making creamy, thick, stable emulsions in small amounts. We tried traditional blenders and full-capacity food processors for making dressings, but those machines aren't well suited for small yields. In addition, we tried smaller "personal" blenders (designed to make a single smoothie) and small food processors, but the immersion blender surpassed them both in performance. Success, though, depends on using a tall, narrow container like the beaker that comes with the blender, which promotes efficient mixing. And because the immersion blender beats all the ingredients into submission, there is no need to dissolve the salt in the liquid as we do with the dressings shaken in jars.

RASP GRATER

Super-sharp rasp-style graters have been on the market for years, and they're the best tool, hands down, for finely grating citrus zest, garlic, ginger, hard cheese, and nutmeg. You should have one.

SMALL WHISK

Though we use a jar to make many dressings, we readily admit when a jar isn't up to the task and it's time to reach for a whisk. The whisk we reach for is small, because our recipe yields and ingredient quantities are modest. A small whisk, about 8 in [20 cm] long, gets ingredients moving in a contained, efficient way in a small bowl. We prefer a stainless-steel one with a solid feel, a substantial (for its size) grippable handle, and numerous wires.

RUBBER AND SILICONE SPATULAS

Made of rubber or heatproof silicone, these tools bend and flex their way into the corners and contours of small jars, efficiently scooping up the remnants of their contents. Standard-size rubber spatulas are great for stirring dressing ingredients and scraping them out of a bowl. Silicone spatulas are heatproof and so are perfect for stirring hot liquids on the stove. Large rubber or silicone spatula-spoons are very useful for tossing delicate greens in a big salad bowl.

TECHNIQUES

Making a great salad involves some prep work, but it's hardly rocket science. There are just a few hows to keep in mind: how to make a vinaigrette, how to season a dressing for a well-balanced salad, how to prep and store your greens, and how to dress your salad.

MAKING A VINAIGRETTE

Within the category of salad dressings is a subset called vinaigrettes. We define a vinaigrette as a mixture of oil and vinegar, though sometimes citrus juice or another acidic ingredient supplements or replaces the vinegar. A vinaigrette is, when mixed and ready to use, an emulsion, which is a blend of two liquids—think oil and vinegar—that wouldn't ordinarily combine. For most types of vinaigrettes, emulsifying the two components depends on breaking down the acidic ingredient into tiny, tiny droplets that will become suspended in the oil, transforming the two into a uniform sauce. Creating the necessary tiny droplets requires mechanical action, or more simply stated, some serious agitation.

This is where technique enters the picture. Since the dawn of salad-dom, the idea has been to combine all the ingredients except for the oil, which you then add gradually and very, very slowly, vigorously whisking all the while. If you've drizzled slowly enough and whisked hard enough, you're rewarded with a silky vinaigrette in which the oil and vinegar are fully integrated.

This technique is tried and true, but there's an easier way: using an impeccably clean, lidded glass jar. We favor adding the ingredients to a jar, tightly sealing the lid, and shaking like crazy, not unlike how a bartender shakes drink ingredients in a cocktail shaker. We do this in two stages. First, swirl the acid(s) and seasonings in the jar to help dissolve the salt (which doesn't dissolve in oil), and then add the oil and shake to make the emulsion.

Some argue that this is a shortcut resulting in a harsher-tasting vinaigrette because the droplets are not as fine or as evenly dispersed as they would be with whisking. But our testing, tasting, and salad making has shown the difference to be slight and, to our palates, imperceptible once the vinaigrette is tossed with the greens.

In addition to being a whole lot easier—and, dare we say, more reliable—than the drizzle-and-whisk routine, using a jar offers several other advantages. First, you don't have to worry about using your third hand—LOL!—to steady the mixing bowl while hand number-one pours and hand number-two whisks. Second, there's no whisk or extra bowls to clean. Third, if you happen to have any leftover vinaigrette, it's already in an airtight container for storage. Fourth, and perhaps most compelling, when the vinaigrette separates, and we guarantee it will because vinaigrette emulsions are unstable, it will come back together easily with just a little more shaking.

BALANCING SEASONINGS AND FLAVORINGS

The classic vinegar-to-oil ratio for a standard vinaigrette is 1 to 3—that is, one part acid to three parts oil. We find that this is really just a suggestion, and we often alter the ratio. Just keep the following in mind: When sampled on a spoon, any dressing—vinaigrette or otherwise—should taste slightly too tangy and acidic, as well

as slightly overseasoned with salt and pepper. The exaggerated flavors are then muted by the greens.

You may notice that many of the recipes in this book call for a sweetener of some sort. In some cases, sweetness is essential to the dressing's taste profile. In other cases, we add a small measure of sugar, honey, or agave to create a lively interplay of flavors, but not necessarily to add a marked sweetness.

WASHING SALAD GREENS

If you make salads frequently and don't own a salad spinner, put down this book now and go purchase one. It will become your new best friend. There is simply no tool as effective as a salad spinner for drying greens after washing—and we cannot overemphasize the importance of well-dried greens to a good salad. Water clinging to leaves not only throws off the balance of the dressing and salad but it also prevents oil-based dressings from coating the leaves because, as we know, oil and water don't mix.

Here are our recommendations for getting the most out of your salad spinner.

- Fill the spinner bowl with water, add the greens, swish them around, and then allow them to soak long enough for any grit to settle. Lift out the greens so that the grit stays at the bottom of the bowl and then pour off the water.

- When spinning dry, work in batches and don't overcrowd the basket. Greens won't dry well if too many are packed together.

- Put the greens through a preliminary spin cycle, lift out the basket, pour off the water in the bowl, redistribute the greens, and spin again. Repeat this process until no more water collects in the bowl. Multiple spin cycles get the greens as dry as they can be.

- Once your greens are dry, pour out any water in the bowl and line the empty spinner basket with a clean, slightly damp kitchen towel or lightly moistened paper towels. Return the greens to the basket and store them, covered, in the spinner in the refrigerator. The basket allows for some air circulation to keep the greens fresh, and the towel will keep them from drying out while absorbing excess moisture.

DRESSING A SALAD

When dressing a salad, our recommendation is to go easy so the greens retain their integrity and don't go listless under the weight of the dressing. Our very general guideline is to use 1 Tbsp of dressing for every 2 cups [30 to 65 g] of greens, but the amount may vary depending on the type of greens, the other salad components, the intensity and consistency of the dressing, and your preference (barely coated to completely drenched).

Delicate greens such as mesclun and baby arugula bruise easily, so use a light touch when tossing; clean hands are the gentlest and most effective tools, so save the tongs for sturdy greens. Here's a tip if you're tossing a large salad: Put half the greens in the mixing bowl, drizzle with some of the dressing, repeat with the remaining greens and dressing, and then toss. This technique helps minimize the degree to which you must handle the greens.

Once your salad is dressed, do a seasoning check by tasting a leaf or two. Even if you carefully seasoned your dressing, you'll likely find that the salad needs a little more salt and pepper. We find that seasoning adjustment is almost a given.

Finally, whether you serve salad American-style as a first course, side dish, or main dish, or whether you hew to the European tradition of serving salad as a post-main course palate cleanser, don't toss fresh greens with dressing in advance of bringing the salad to the table (the exception is raw kale salad; see page 64). Wait until the last possible moment so the leaves stay lively and perky.

A salad dressing that has been stored in the refrigerator should be brought to room temperature before use. This is easily accomplished by allowing it to stand on the counter for about 30 minutes, or by placing it, in its container, in a bowl of tepid water for 10 to 15 minutes. The Browned Butter Vinaigrette (page 72) and Bacon–Black Pepper Vinaigrette (page 71) should be warmed, uncovered, either in the microwave (for 20 to 30 seconds, stirring once or twice); in a small skillet over medium-low heat; or by placing the jar in a bowl of hot water for a few minutes. Once the dressing is fluid, give it a good shake or stir to recombine. Because a vinaigrette is a very unstable emulsion, if it's left to stand for even just a few minutes, it will need to be recombined before use. So make sure to shake or whisk seconds before you dress your salad. Most of the dressings in this book can be stored for up to 3 days; Pomegranate Molasses–Walnut Oil Vinaigrette (page 54) and Miso Dressing with Ginger and Orange (page 61) will keep for up to 1 week.

THE GARLIC RUB

The technique for making a classic Caesar salad includes rubbing the salad bowl with a clove of garlic. Is this just a romantic salad ritual, or is there something to this step?

As garlic lovers, we buy into this romantic ritual. You won't get in-your-face flavor by rubbing the bowl with a garlic clove, but you will get a subtle aroma that can add nuance to a simple salad. If you try this technique, choose a salad bowl that has some texture on its interior surface—a wooden bowl is great, as is a ceramic bowl with a rough glaze, or even a much-used stainless-steel bowl with scratches. Halve the garlic clove, and then lightly smash the halves with the side of a chef's knife to get the juices flowing. Rub the cut side of the garlic clove all over the inside of the bowl, pressing firmly as you go. If you like, rub your salad-tossing utensils, too.

CLASSIC FRENCH VINAIGRETTE

Extra-virgin olive oil, wine vinegar, mustard, shallot, salt, and pepper—these are the building blocks of a classic French vinaigrette. There is nothing new or innovative about this formula, and it proves once again that new isn't necessarily better. This vinaigrette is as satisfying today as the day it was first conceived. Tarragon—we like 2 tsp of chopped fresh—is a tried-and-true, common flavor addition, if you're so inclined.

MAKES ABOUT ½ CUP [120 ML]

1½ Tbsp red or white wine vinegar

1 tsp Dijon mustard

2 Tbsp minced shallot

Kosher salt

Freshly ground black pepper

⅓ cup [80 ml] extra-virgin olive oil

In a glass jar, combine the vinegar, mustard, shallot, ½ tsp salt, and ¼ tsp pepper and swirl to dissolve the salt. Add the olive oil, tightly screw on the lid, and shake until the ingredients are well combined. Let stand to allow the flavors to meld, about 15 minutes. Taste and adjust the seasoning with additional salt and pepper, if necessary. Shake to recombine just before using.

EXTRAS

Familiar salad companions—tomatoes, radishes, cucumber, celery, fennel, bell pepper, artichoke hearts, olives, poached egg, crumbled cooked bacon

SERVE ON:

Any type of lettuce or salad greens

Asparagus

Green beans

Thin slices of raw or cooked beet or carrot

APPLE CIDER, GRAINY MUSTARD, AND SHALLOT VINAIGRETTE

Apple cider, when reduced on the stove, has a nice viscosity and acidity, but it's quite sweet, so we balance it with apple cider vinegar, rustic whole-grain mustard, and mildly pungent shallots. While it's terrific on a sturdy salad, honestly, we'd eat this autumnal vinaigrette plain by the spoonful!

SERVE ON:

Any type of lettuce or salad greens

Brassicas (Lacinato kale, roasted Brussels sprouts, cooked cabbage)

Roasted winter squash

Roasted root vegetables (beets, carrots, celery root, parsnips, turnips)

Roasted sweet potatoes

MAKES ABOUT ¾ CUP [180 ML]

¾ cup [180 ml] apple cider or unfiltered apple juice
2 Tbsp apple cider vinegar, preferably raw unfiltered
3 Tbsp minced shallot
Kosher salt
Freshly ground black pepper
1½ Tbsp whole-grain Dijon mustard
¼ cup [60 ml] mild-flavored extra-virgin olive oil

In a small skillet over medium-high heat, bring the cider to a boil. Continue boiling, swirling the pan occasionally, until reduced to 3 Tbsp, about 5 minutes. Pour the hot reduced cider into a heat-proof glass jar and let cool to room temperature.

Add the vinegar, shallot, ½ tsp salt, and ¼ tsp pepper to the jar and swirl to dissolve the salt. Add the mustard and olive oil, screw on the lid tightly, and shake until the ingredients are well combined. Let stand to allow the flavors to meld, about 15 minutes. Taste and adjust the seasoning with additional salt and pepper, if necessary. Shake to recombine just before using.

EXTRAS
Fennel, radishes, kohlrabi, apple, pear, persimmon, toasted nuts (walnuts, hazelnuts, pecans, almonds), barley, farro, wild rice, fresh goat cheese, aged Cheddar cheese, blue cheese, smoked ham

CITRUS,
HONEY, AND
ROSEMARY
VINAIGRETTE

With an eye toward a subtle rosemary presence in this vinaigrette, we use just a little rosemary and call the immersion blender to duty to really batter it, to maximize its fragrance and flavor. Floral sweetness from the honey, resinous tones from the rosemary, and bright citrus notes harmonize into a balanced vinaigrette that complements every type of lettuce.

MAKES ABOUT ⅔ CUP [160 ML]

1½ Tbsp rice vinegar

1 Tbsp honey

1½ tsp chopped fresh rosemary

1 tsp finely grated orange zest

½ tsp finely grated lemon zest,
plus 1½ tsp fresh lemon juice

Kosher salt

Freshly ground black pepper

⅓ cup [80 ml] extra-virgin olive oil

2 Tbsp minced shallot

In the beaker of an immersion blender, combine the vinegar, honey, rosemary, orange zest, lemon zest, lemon juice, ½ tsp salt, ¼ tsp pepper, and olive oil. Purée until the rosemary is broken down and fragrant and the vinaigrette is smooth. Add the shallot and stir to combine. Let stand to allow the flavors to meld, about 15 minutes. Taste and adjust the seasoning with additional salt and pepper, if necessary. Briskly stir to recombine just before using.

SERVE ON:

Any type of lettuce

Mesclun

Escarole

Endive

Fennel

Summer squash

Roasted root vegetables
(beets, carrots, parsnips)

Roasted sweet potatoes

EXTRAS

Roasted bell peppers, tomatoes, pears, figs, grapes, orange, grapefruit, fresh goat cheese, Petit Basque cheese, Manchego cheese

FRESH MINT
VINAIGRETTE

Fresh mint lends a gentle tingle to this vinaigrette. Most supermarkets stock spearmint, which has a relatively sweet flavor and mild menthol hit. Peppermint has a deeper, spicier, more peppery (hence the name) flavor and smaller, darker green leaves. Either works well here, but if you can grow, or otherwise get your hands on, some peppermint, it's our first choice. The mint loses some vibrancy as the vinaigrette sits for a few hours, so make the dressing right before using.

SERVE ON:

- Lettuce (romaine, red, green leaf lettuce, butter)
- Endive
- Asparagus
- Green beans
- Grilled or roasted eggplant
- Summer squash
- Roasted root vegetables (winter squash, sweet potatoes, beets)

MAKES ABOUT ½ CUP [120 ML]

1½ Tbsp rice vinegar

1 tsp fresh lemon juice

1 tsp sugar

2 Tbsp minced shallot

Kosher salt

Freshly ground black pepper

⅓ cup [80 ml] mild-flavored extra-virgin olive oil

⅓ cup [15 g] finely chopped fresh mint

In a glass jar, combine the vinegar, lemon juice, sugar, shallot, ½ tsp salt, and ¼ tsp pepper and swirl to dissolve the salt. Add the olive oil and mint, screw on the lid tightly, and shake until the ingredients are well combined. Let stand to allow the flavors to meld, about 15 minutes. Taste and adjust the seasoning with additional salt and pepper, if necessary. Shake to recombine and use immediately.

EXTRAS | Raw or roasted carrots, pickled shallot, pickled red onion, tomatoes, roasted red peppers, apple, orange, grapefruit, Israeli couscous, fava beans, feta cheese

This elegant vinaigrette balances fruitiness, sweetness, nuttiness, and tanginess. It gets its creamy, luxe consistency from the pear, which acts as an emulsifying agent. Use any variety of pear you like. What's important is that the fruit is fully ripe and has a custardy texture; a knife should glide through the flesh.

We like this dressing made with shallot as much as we like it without. With it, the sweet notes are tempered by the shallot's pungency; without it, the honeyed flavors are front and center. We leave it up to you to decide.

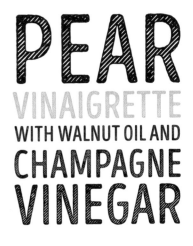

PEAR
VINAIGRETTE
WITH WALNUT OIL AND
CHAMPAGNE
VINEGAR

MAKES ABOUT ½ CUP [120 ML]

½ ripe medium pear, peeled, cored, and roughly diced

2½ Tbsp toasted walnut oil

1½ Tbsp mild-flavored extra-virgin olive oil

2 Tbsp champagne vinegar

1½ tsp honey

1 Tbsp minced shallot (optional)

Kosher salt

Freshly ground black pepper

In the beaker of an immersion blender, combine the pear, walnut oil, olive oil, vinegar, honey, shallot (if using), ¾ tsp salt, and ½ tsp pepper. Purée until smooth. Let stand to allow the flavors to meld, about 15 minutes. Taste and adjust the seasoning with additional salt and pepper, if necessary. Briskly stir to recombine just before using.

EXTRAS

Toasted nuts (walnuts, hazelnuts, pistachios), cooked peeled chestnuts, dried figs, dried cranberries, dried cherries, fresh goat cheese, Parmigiano-Reggiano cheese, blue cheese, freshly ground black pepper

SERVE ON:

Romaine

Red or green leaf lettuce

Radicchio

Endive

Frisée

Roasted Brussels sprouts

Fennel

Roasted winter squash

Roasted turnips

PINEAPPLE, CORIANDER, AND LIME
VINAIGRETTE

Because coriander has distinct citrusy tones, it makes a great partner for fruit. In this vinaigrette, lime picks up the tart end of the bargain, while pineapple imparts its hallmark tropical, tangy sweetness. We prefer the texture of finely chopped pineapple here, but if you would like these same flavors in a smoother format, whiz the ingredients with an immersion blender.

MAKES ABOUT ⅔ CUP [160 ML]

1½ Tbsp fresh lime juice

1½ tsp honey or light agave nectar

1 tsp ground coriander

1 medium garlic clove, germ removed (see page 13), grated or minced to a paste

Kosher salt

Freshly ground black pepper

⅓ cup [70 g] finely chopped fresh pineapple

⅓ cup [80 ml] mild-flavored extra-virgin olive oil

In a glass jar, combine the lime juice, honey, coriander, garlic, ½ tsp salt, and ¼ tsp pepper and swirl to dissolve the salt. Add the pineapple and olive oil, screw on the lid tightly, and shake until the ingredients are well combined. Let stand to allow the flavors to meld, about 15 minutes. Taste and adjust the seasoning with additional salt and pepper, if necessary. Shake to recombine just before using.

SERVE ON:

- Romaine
- Green leaf lettuce
- Arugula
- Baby kale
- Shredded cabbage
- Roasted sweet potatoes
- Grilled meats (chicken, pork tenderloin)
- Grilled or seared meaty white fish (such as halibut)
- Grilled shrimp

EXTRAS Grilled or raw onions, bell peppers, cucumber, jicama, grape or cherry tomatoes, pickled jalapeños, roasted green chiles, avocado, green onions, cilantro, quinoa, toasted coconut, roasted peanuts

PINEAPPLE VINAIGRETTE WITH MINT AND CHILE

Add 3 Tbsp finely chopped fresh mint and 1½ tsp minced serrano chile (with or without seeds and membranes, depending on how much heat you want) along with the pineapple and olive oil, and proceed as directed.

Originally from South Africa, Peppadews are small, bright red chiles that have been cored, seeded, and packed in brine, like pickles. They've taken the American market by storm, and with good reason—they're mighty appealing little bites with rollicking, wide-ranging flavor, from fruity to tangy and sweet to hot. Both hot and mild Peppadews are available in many supermarkets now, and we went with hot ones here. If you'd prefer a mellower vinaigrette, just switch to the mild variety.

SHARP-AND-SWEET-
WITH-A-LITTLE-BIT-OF-HEAT
PEPPADEW
VINAIGRETTE

MAKES ABOUT ⅔ CUP [160 ML]

1 Tbsp Peppadew packing liquid,
plus ¼ cup [60 g] minced hot Peppadews

2 tsp sherry vinegar

1 tsp honey or light agave nectar

1 medium garlic clove, germ removed (see page 13),
grated or minced to a paste

Kosher salt

Freshly ground black pepper

⅓ cup [80 ml] extra-virgin olive oil

In a glass jar, combine the Peppadew packing liquid, vinegar, honey, garlic, ½ tsp salt, and ¼ tsp pepper and swirl to dissolve the salt. Add the minced Peppadews and olive oil, screw on the lid tightly, and shake until the ingredients are well combined. Let stand to allow the flavors to meld, about 15 minutes. Taste and adjust the seasoning with additional salt and pepper, if necessary. Shake to recombine just before using.

EXTRAS

Fennel, cucumber, jicama, grilled corn, grape or cherry tomatoes, avocado, mango, Israeli couscous, quinoa, barley, black beans, fresh goat cheese, Manchego cheese

SERVE ON:

Romaine

Red or green leaf lettuce

Butter lettuce

Escarole

Frisée

Endive

Baby kale

Spinach

Shredded cabbage

Roasted or steamed
broccoli or Broccolini

Roasted cauliflower

Grilled eggplant

Summer squash

Roasted winter squash

Roasted beets

SWEET AND TANGY CHIA SEED DRESSING

Classic poppy-seed dressing gets a makeover with chia seeds. The tiny seeds are celebrated as a superfood, thanks to the omega-3s they contain. Chia seeds have a gelling quality, so if you want a thin dressing for delicate greens, use the dressing right after mixing. But if you're after a thicker consistency to coat sturdy lettuces, let the mixture stand for about 30 minutes before using. Toasting chia seeds gives them a subtle walnut-like flavor, but you can skip this step if you're pressed for time.

MAKES ⅔ CUP [160 ML]

1 Tbsp chia seeds

3 Tbsp apple cider vinegar, preferably raw unfiltered

1½ Tbsp light agave nectar

¾ tsp Dijon mustard

Kosher salt

Freshly ground black pepper

⅓ cup [80 ml] neutral oil, such as safflower, sunflower, or canola

In a small skillet over medium heat, toast the chia seeds, stirring frequently, until they turn shiny and the light-colored ones are a few shades darker, about 5 minutes. Transfer to a small plate and let cool completely.

In a glass jar, combine the vinegar, agave nectar, mustard, ½ tsp salt, and ¼ tsp pepper and swirl to dissolve the salt. Add the chia seeds and oil, screw on the lid tightly, and shake until the ingredients are well combined. Taste and adjust the seasoning with additional salt and pepper, if needed. Use immediately or, if you prefer a slightly thicker consistency, let stand for about 30 minutes and shake to recombine just before using.

SERVE ON:

IF USING RIGHT AWAY

- Red or green leaf lettuce
- Butter lettuce
- Mesclun
- Baby kale
- Spinach

IF ALLOWING TO THICKEN

- Romaine
- Escarole
- Lacinato kale
- Sliced tomatoes

EXTRAS

Apple, pear, toasted nuts (walnuts, pecans, almonds), sweet onion, cucumber, radishes, celery, avocado, Pecorino Romano cheese, Manchego cheese

CARROT-GINGER DRESSING WITH SOY AND SESAME

When you toss your greens with this vibrant Asian-accented dressing, you're saucing your vegetables with vegetables! A small measure of white miso adds umami notes that make the flavors deeper and fuller, but you can opt out of the miso and the dressing will still taste great. Any type of onion—red, white, or yellow—works here, so use what you have on hand.

MAKES ABOUT ⅔ CUP [160 ML]

½ cup [70 g] peeled and chopped carrot

1 Tbsp chopped onion

3 Tbsp neutral oil, such as
safflower, sunflower, or canola

2 Tbsp rice vinegar

1½ tsp soy sauce

½ tsp toasted sesame oil

1 tsp sugar

1 tsp grated peeled fresh ginger

1 tsp white miso (optional)

¼ tsp freshly ground white pepper

Kosher salt

In the beaker of an immersion blender, combine the carrot, onion, oil, vinegar, soy sauce, sesame oil, sugar, ginger, miso (if using), pepper, and ¼ tsp salt. Purée until the mixture is as smooth as possible (it will still have a slightly pulpy texture). Taste and adjust the seasoning with additional salt, if necessary. Let stand to allow the flavors to meld, about 15 minutes. Briskly stir to recombine just before using.

EXTRAS

Radishes, bell peppers, thinly sliced onion, daikon sprouts, green onions, toasted sesame seeds

SERVE ON:

Romaine

Red or green leaf lettuce

Spinach

Baby kale

Shredded cabbage

Cucumber

Summer squash

Roasted or grilled eggplant

Roasted golden beets

Roasted or grilled okra

MANGO– RED CURRY
DRESSING

This dressing captures the hot, sour, salty, sweet flavors that are characteristic of Thai food, and we add fruitiness, too. Mango gives the dressing a lush smoothness. Either fresh or thawed frozen mango works well, but if you're using fresh, make sure the fruit is fully ripe— it should be fragrant and yield to gentle pressure.

SERVE ON:

- Romaine
- Green leaf lettuce
- Shredded cabbage
- Roasted or steamed broccoli or Broccolini
- Grilled salmon, shrimp, or pork
- Seared duck breasts

MAKES ABOUT ½ CUP [120 ML]

1½ tsp Thai red curry paste

1½ Tbsp neutral oil, such as safflower, sunflower, or canola

½ cup [70 g] fresh or thawed frozen mango chunks

1½ Tbsp fresh lime juice

2 tsp fish sauce

1½ tsp sugar, plus more as needed

Kosher salt (optional)

In a small skillet over medium heat, combine the curry paste and 1½ tsp of the oil and stir to mix. Cook the mixture (it should sizzle lightly after about 1 minute), stirring and mashing it with a silicone spatula, until the curry paste is slightly darker in color, dryish, and very fragrant, 3 to 4 minutes. Set aside to let cool.

In the beaker of an immersion blender, combine the mango, lime juice, fish sauce, sugar, the remaining 1 Tbsp oil, and the curry paste–oil mixture. Purée until the mixture is smooth. Taste and adjust the seasoning, adding salt and more sugar, if necessary. Let stand to allow the flavors to meld, about 15 minutes. Stir to recombine just before using.

EXTRAS

Carrots, bell peppers, sliced red onion, steamed or sautéed snow peas, grape or cherry tomatoes, jicama, cilantro, green onions, fresh mint, toasted sesame seeds, toasted unsweetened coconut

A key ingredient in Mexican and American Southwestern cooking, tomatillos have a compelling tart, slightly grassy flavor that gives dishes brightness and dimension. But this flavor can run wild if left unchecked, which is why we use just a single tomatillo in this dressing and char it in a dry pan (cast iron is wonderful for this). The charring softens the flavor and highlights the earthy notes, helping the tomatillo to harmonize with the cilantro, garlic, fresh chile, and lime in the dressing. Just a touch of honey or agave syrup brings the dressing into balance.

CHARRED TOMATILLO AND CILANTRO DRESSING

MAKES ABOUT ¾ CUP [180 ML]

6 oz [170 g] tomatillo(s), husked and halved

1½ Tbsp fresh lime juice

1 Tbsp honey or light agave nectar

¼ cup [10 g] chopped fresh cilantro

1½ tsp minced seeded serrano chile

1 medium garlic clove, germ removed (see page 13), grated or minced to a paste

3 Tbsp extra-virgin olive oil

Kosher salt

Freshly ground black pepper

In a small cast-iron or nonstick skillet over medium heat, place the tomatillo halves, cut-side down, and cook, undisturbed, until charred, about 10 minutes. Transfer to the beaker of an immersion blender and let cool slightly.

Add the lime juice, honey, cilantro, chile, garlic, olive oil, ½ tsp salt, and ¼ tsp pepper to the beaker. Purée with the immersion blender until the mixture is smooth. Let stand to allow the flavors to meld, about 15 minutes. Taste and adjust the seasoning, adding additional salt and pepper if necessary. Briskly stir to recombine just before using.

EXTRAS

Roasted green chiles, jicama, avocado, peaches, mango, orange, black beans, roasted salted pepitas (shelled pumpkin seeds), queso fresco

SERVE ON:

Romaine

Green leaf lettuce

Shredded cabbage

Summer squash

Grilled corn

Grilled bell pepper and onion

Grilled or sautéed shrimp, salmon, or white fish

Grilled or roasted chicken

ESCAROLE SALAD WITH TANGERINES, MARCONA ALMONDS, AND CITRUS, HONEY, AND ROSEMARY VINAIGRETTE

SERVES 4 AS A SALAD COURSE OR SIDE DISH

This salad is bright and refreshing and is as lovely to behold as it is to eat. Marcona almonds—small, flattish, richly flavorful almonds from Spain that are traditionally fried—are available in well-stocked markets and specialty stores. Regular almonds that have been deeply toasted are fine stand-ins. Whichever you use, chop the nuts but leave them in large pieces so they add lots of texture. Manchego cheese is optional, but its saltiness is a nice counterpoint to the sweetness of the tangerines and citrus vinaigrette.

8 cups [120 g] torn escarole leaves

¼ cup [60 ml] Citrus, Honey, and Rosemary Vinaigrette (page 29), plus more as needed

Kosher salt

Freshly ground black pepper

4 small or 3 medium seedless tangerines, such as clementines or satsumas, peeled and separated into segments

¼ cup [35 g] Marcona almonds, very coarsely chopped

Small wedge of Manchego cheese for shaving (optional)

Put the escarole in a large bowl and drizzle with 3 Tbsp of the vinaigrette and toss to coat. Taste and adjust the seasoning and add more dressing, if necessary. Transfer the dressed greens to a serving platter.

Put the tangerine segments in the large bowl, drizzle with a spoonful of the vinaigrette, toss to coat, and scatter them over the greens. Sprinkle the almonds over the top. Using a vegetable peeler, shave the Manchego cheese directly onto the salad, if desired, and drizzle a spoonful of vinaigrette over the salad, allowing the dressing to fall onto the cheese. Serve immediately.

BRUSSELS SPROUTS AND APPLE SALAD WITH GOAT CHEESE AND
CIDER-GRAINY MUSTARD VINAIGRETTE

SERVES 4 TO 6 AS A SALAD COURSE OR SIDE DISH

This salad screams "autumn!" But now that Brussels sprouts are available year-round, you can make it during any season you'd like. There's no denying that putting this dish together requires more than just a little prep, but with layers of contrasting flavors, an intriguing interplay of textures, and lovely shapes and colors, it's a special salad—one that's perfect for the holiday table.

The goal when roasting the Brussels sprouts is to get a mixture of browned, tender pieces and crisp, darkly charred (some would say burnt) bits. Don't be shy about letting the sprouts color deeply—doing so brings out their best flavor and aroma.

3 Tbsp golden raisins

2 Tbsp apple cider vinegar, warmed

1½ lb [680 g] Brussels sprouts

2 Tbsp neutral oil, such as safflower, sunflower, or canola

Kosher salt

Freshly ground black pepper

1 medium crisp apple, such as Gala, Fuji, or Braeburn

½ lemon

1 cup [12 g] packed flat-leaf parsley leaves, torn if large

3½ Tbsp Apple Cider, Grainy Mustard, and Shallot Vinaigrette (page 26), plus more as needed

½ cup [55 g] fresh goat cheese, crumbled

In a small bowl or a ramekin, stir together the raisins and warm vinegar and set aside to plump up and cool.

Adjust an oven rack to the center position, set a rimmed baking sheet on the rack, and preheat the oven to 500°F [260°C].

Trim about ⅜ in [1 cm] off the bottom of each Brussels sprout, remove and discard any blemished outer leaves, and reserve any good leaves that fall off in the process. Slice each sprout from top to bottom into rounds no thicker than ¼ in [6 mm]. In a large bowl, toss the sliced sprouts and loose leaves, the oil, 1 tsp salt, and ½ tsp pepper until the sprouts are evenly coated.

Carefully remove the hot baking sheet from the oven and empty the sprouts onto it, distributing them in an even layer. Return the baking sheet to the oven and roast the sprouts, stirring two or three times, until they are a mixture of crisp, darkly charred bits and tender green slices, about 15 minutes. Let cool to room temperature on the baking sheet.

Continued

While the sprouts are cooling, use an apple corer to punch out the apple core and use a paring knife to halve the fruit lengthwise. (If you don't have a corer, halve the apple lengthwise and notch out the core from each half with a paring knife.) Cut each half crosswise into ⅛-in [4-mm] slices; discard (or eat) the end pieces. Put the apple slices into a medium bowl, squeeze in 2 to 3 tsp juice from the lemon half, and toss to coat to help prevent the apple from discoloring.

Pour off and discard the unabsorbed vinegar from the raisins.

Transfer the cooled Brussels sprouts to a large bowl. Add the raisins, apple slices, and parsley leaves and drizzle with the dressing. Using a large rubber spatula, gently toss to combine, separating any apple slices that stick together. Taste and adjust the seasoning and add more dressing, if necessary, and toss again. Scatter the goat cheese over the top and gently toss once or twice to distribute. Transfer to a serving platter and serve immediately.

SLAW WITH RED BELL PEPPER, ORANGE, GRILLED SHRIMP, AND CHARRED TOMATILLO AND CILANTRO DRESSING

SERVES 4 AS A MAIN COURSE

Salting and then letting the cabbage rest softens it and draws out some excess liquid. After rinsing and drying, it will be compacted—just fluff it up with a fork or your fingers. To prevent the shrimp from sticking, we oil both the shrimp and the grill grate. Shrimp can overcook in a flash, so watch them like a hawk. The smaller the shrimp, the greater the risk of overcooking, which is why we specify extra-large shrimp. If you'd like them smaller, once they're cool enough to handle, halve each one lengthwise.

1¼ lb [570 g] green cabbage, cored and finely shredded

Kosher salt

1¼ lb [570 g] extra-large shrimp (26/30), peeled, deveined, rinsed, dried, and threaded onto skewers

Neutral oil, such as sunflower, safflower, or canola, for brushing

Freshly ground black pepper

½ cup [120 ml] Charred Tomatillo and Cilantro Dressing (page 41), plus more as needed

1 medium red bell pepper, cored, seeded, and thinly sliced

1 large navel orange, peeled, sectioned, and each section cut crosswise into 5 pieces

4 medium green onions, white and green parts, thinly sliced

In a colander or large mesh strainer set over a medium bowl, toss the cabbage with 1 Tbsp salt until well combined. Let stand until the cabbage wilts slightly, at least 1 hour or up to 4 hours. Rinse the cabbage under very cold running water and drain well. Dry the cabbage with a clean kitchen towel or in a salad spinner, and transfer to a large bowl. (At this point, you can cover it and refrigerate for up to 3 days.)

Prepare a hot fire in a charcoal grill or preheat a gas grill on high for 15 minutes.

Brush the skewered shrimp with oil and sprinkle lightly with salt and pepper. Clean and oil the grill grate. Grill the shrimp (covered, if using a gas grill) until just opaque and pink, turning as necessary, 3 to 4 minutes. Remove the shrimp from the skewers to a large bowl, add about 2 Tbsp of the dressing, and toss to coat.

In another large bowl, toss the cabbage, bell pepper, orange pieces, most of the green onions, ¼ tsp salt, and ½ tsp black pepper with the remaining dressing until well coated. Taste and adjust the seasoning, if necessary, and place in a bed on a large serving platter. Arrange the shrimp over the slaw, sprinkle with the remaining green onions, and serve immediately.

MAPLE-MUSTARD VINAIGRETTE

Maple paired with a gentle hint of garlic, just enough mustard to let you know it's there, and white balsamic vinegar that echoes the sweetness of the syrup is a crowd-pleasing combo. We go for Grade A Dark and Robust syrup, which is roughly equivalent to the former Grade B syrup. If you don't have white balsamic on hand, try apple cider vinegar— it's not quite as sweet, but has a fruity quality that complements the maple. And if you like the pop of whole mustard seeds, substitute whole-grain Dijon for the garden-variety type.

MAKES ABOUT ½ CUP [120 ML]

1½ Tbsp pure maple syrup, preferably Grade A Dark and Robust

2 Tbsp white balsamic vinegar

1 medium garlic clove, germ removed (see page 13), grated or minced to a paste

Kosher salt

Freshly ground black pepper

1 Tbsp Dijon mustard

¼ cup [60 ml] extra-virgin olive oil

In a glass jar, combine the maple syrup, vinegar, garlic, ½ tsp salt, and ¼ tsp pepper and swirl to dissolve the salt. Add the mustard and olive oil, screw on the lid tightly, and shake until the ingredients are well combined. Let stand to allow the flavors to meld, about 15 minutes. Taste and adjust the seasoning with additional salt and pepper, if necessary. Shake to recombine just before using.

EXTRAS

Carrots, cucumber, onion, apple, pear, orange, toasted nuts (walnuts, hazelnuts, pecans, almonds), Parmigiano-Reggiano cheese, sharp Cheddar cheese, crumbled cooked bacon

MAPLE-MUSTARD-HAZELNUT VINAIGRETTE

Substitute 2 Tbsp each toasted hazelnut oil and neutral oil (such as safflower, sunflower, or canola) for the extra-virgin olive oil and proceed as directed.

SERVE ON:

- Romaine
- Red or green leaf lettuce
- Butter lettuce
- Escarole
- Frisée
- Endive
- Spinach
- Lacinato kale
- Roasted Brussels sprouts
- Roasted winter squash
- Roasted root vegetables (beets, carrots, parsnips, turnips)
- Grilled or roasted pork

BLACK OLIVE-
BALSAMIC
VINAIGRETTE

Kalamata olives are salty, silky, and sultry, and your larder should never be without them. We've eaten plenty of salads that include Kalamatas, but rarely in the dressing itself. We like this approach because it spreads the distinctive flavor to every corner of the salad.

MAKES ABOUT ⅔ CUP [160 ML]

2 Tbsp white balsamic vinegar

1 medium garlic clove, germ removed (see page 13), grated or minced to a paste

1 tsp finely grated lemon zest

Pinch of red pepper flakes (optional)

Kosher salt

Freshly ground black pepper

⅓ cup [45 g] Kalamata olives, pitted and minced

⅓ cup [80 ml] extra-virgin olive oil

In a glass jar, combine the vinegar, garlic, lemon zest, red pepper flakes (if using), ½ tsp salt, and ¼ tsp black pepper and swirl to dissolve the salt. Add the olives and olive oil, screw on the lid tightly, and shake until the ingredients are well combined. Let stand to allow the flavors to meld, about 15 minutes. Taste and adjust the seasoning with additional salt and black pepper, if necessary. Shake to recombine just before using.

EXTRAS **Raw or roasted bell peppers, grape or cherry tomatoes, oranges, white beans, chickpeas, Israeli couscous, fresh basil, fresh parsley, toasted pine nuts, fresh goat cheese, feta cheese, mozzarella cheese, anchovies, hard-cooked eggs**

BLACK OLIVE, BALSAMIC, AND BASIL VINAIGRETTE

Add 3 Tbsp finely chopped fresh basil along with the olives and olive oil, and proceed as directed. Basil discolors pretty quickly, so use this vinaigrette when it's freshly made.

SERVE ON:

- Romaine
- Red or green leaf lettuce
- Spinach
- Grilled or roasted onions
- Fennel
- Summer squash
- Sliced tomatoes
- Roasted root vegetables (beets, carrots, potatoes, sweet potatoes)
- Artichoke hearts
- Grilled or seared fish
- Grilled or roasted lamb

They say—and they're right about this—that you should replace your spices annually so they'll be fresh and flavorful. For us, this happens naturally with smoked paprika, a.k.a. pimentón. We love it, and go through it quickly. Available in sweet, bittersweet, and hot types, we use either sweet or bittersweet to impart its hallmark smoky inflection to this vinaigrette, which gets additional layers of flavor from garlic, shallot, and a hint of pungent Dijon mustard.

SMOKED PAPRIKA VINAIGRETTE

MAKES ABOUT ½ CUP [120 ML]

⅓ cup [80 ml] extra-virgin olive oil

2 tsp sweet or bittersweet smoked paprika

1 medium garlic clove, germ removed (see page 13), grated or minced to a paste

Kosher salt

1½ Tbsp sherry vinegar

1 tsp honey or light agave nectar

Freshly ground black pepper

¾ tsp Dijon mustard

2 Tbsp minced shallot

In a small skillet over medium-low heat, warm the olive oil. Add the paprika, garlic, and a pinch of salt and cook, stirring occasionally, until fragrant and the garlic just begins to sizzle, about 4 minutes. Set the pan aside off the heat to infuse the oil, about 15 minutes. Strain the oil, pressing on the solids to release as much infused oil as possible. Discard the solids.

In a glass jar, combine the vinegar, honey, ½ tsp salt, and ¼ tsp pepper and swirl to dissolve the salt. Add the mustard, shallots, and infused oil; screw on the lid tightly; and shake until the ingredients are well combined. Let stand to allow the flavors to meld, about 15 minutes. Taste and adjust the seasoning with additional salt and pepper, if necessary. Shake to recombine just before using.

EXTRAS

Roasted bell peppers, grilled corn, oranges, figs, dates, toasted almonds or hazelnuts, chickpeas, white beans, farro, Israeli couscous, lentils, queso fresco, mozzarella cheese, Manchego cheese, Spanish-style chorizo

SERVE ON:

Romaine

Green leaf lettuce

Spinach

Baby kale

Roasted cauliflower

Braised leeks

Sautéed chard

Braised collard greens

Grilled or roasted onions or asparagus

Roasted root vegetables (beets, carrots, celery root, parsnips, turnips)

Grilled or roasted pork

Grilled swordfish, squid, or shrimp

POMEGRANATE MOLASSES- WALNUT OIL VINAIGRETTE

With flavors inspired by the Middle East, this vinaigrette is intense, tart-sweet, and full-bodied. Pomegranate molasses is a dark, thick syrup made from pomegranate juice reduced with sugar; it can be found in the international aisle of well-stocked grocery stores and in Middle Eastern markets. Whisking, not shaking, is the best mixing technique for this dressing because of the viscosity of both the pomegranate molasses and the honey.

MAKES ABOUT ½ CUP [120 ML]

1 Tbsp pomegranate molasses

1 Tbsp honey

2 tsp fresh lemon juice

Generous ½ tsp kosher salt

⅛ tsp freshly ground black pepper

3 Tbsp mild-flavored extra-virgin olive oil

2 Tbsp toasted walnut oil

SERVE ON:

- Romaine
- Green leaf lettuce
- Shredded cabbage
- Grilled or roasted onions
- Summer squash
- Grilled eggplant
- Roasted winter squash
- Roasted root vegetables (beets, carrots, parsnips, turnips)
- Seared duck breast
- Grilled or roasted lamb

In a small bowl, whisk the pomegranate molasses, honey, lemon juice, salt, and pepper until well combined and the salt dissolves. (Because this vinaigrette contains very little liquid in the form of vinegar or citrus juice, make sure the salt fully dissolves before adding the oil.) Add the olive oil and walnut oil and whisk until thickened and emulsified. Whisk again to recombine just before using.

EXTRAS

Cucumber, kohlrabi, apples, figs, plums, grapes, pomegranate arils, dates, bulgur, wild rice, farro, toasted walnuts, ricotta salata

SPICED POMEGRANATE MOLASSES- WALNUT OIL VINAIGRETTE

Whisk ¼ tsp ground cumin, ⅛ tsp ground coriander, and ⅛ tsp ground cinnamon into the pomegranate molasses mixture before adding the oils, and proceed as directed.

Caramelized sugar is a flavoring used in Vietnamese cooking, and one that inspired this dressing. We matched bittersweet caramel with fresh orange juice, fragrant shallot, and woodsy sherry vinegar to create a vinaigrette with incredible complexity—sweetness, savoriness, tartness, fruitiness, and a hint of smokiness.

ORANGE, CARAMEL, AND SHERRY VINEGAR VINAIGRETTE

MAKES ABOUT ⅔ CUP [160 ML]

2 Tbsp sugar

2 tsp water

⅓ cup [80 ml] fresh orange juice

1 Tbsp minced shallot

2 Tbsp sherry vinegar

1 tsp Dijon mustard

Kosher salt

Freshly ground black pepper

3 Tbsp mild-flavored extra-virgin olive oil

In a small, heavy-bottomed saucepan over medium-high heat, bring the sugar and water to a simmer, occasionally swirling the pan to help the sugar dissolve. Turn the heat to medium and continue to simmer, frequently swirling the pan, until the sugar is deep amber in color and wisps of smoke appear, about 8 minutes. (Tilting the pan may make it easier to check on the color.)

Remove the pan from the heat and immediately but slowly and carefully add the orange juice and shallot; the liquid will spit and sputter vigorously. Return the pan to medium heat and bring to a simmer, stirring constantly to dissolve the hardened caramel into the liquid, and cook until the mixture is reduced to ¼ cup [60 ml]. Pour the mixture into a heatproof glass jar and let cool.

Add the vinegar, mustard, ½ tsp salt, and ¼ tsp pepper to the jar and swirl to dissolve the salt. Add the olive oil, screw on the lid tightly, and shake until the ingredients are well combined. Let stand to allow the flavors to meld, about 15 minutes. Taste and adjust the seasoning with additional salt and pepper, if necessary. Shake to recombine just before using.

SERVE ON:

Any type of lettuce or salad greens

Green beans

Roasted or grilled asparagus

Roasted cauliflower, broccoli, or Broccolini

Roasted winter squash

Roasted root vegetables (beets, carrots, parsnips, sweet potatoes, turnips)

Grilled or roasted pork or chicken

Seared duck

EXTRAS

Grilled or roasted onions, fennel, apple, pear, grapes, figs, toasted nuts (almonds, hazelnuts, pistachios), wild rice, farro, fresh goat cheese, Parmigiano-Reggiano cheese, Petit Basque cheese

Sumac, a common spice in Middle Eastern cuisines, is ground from the dark reddish-brown berries of the sumac shrub. The flavor is fruity, slightly woodsy, and—moreover—tart. Not surprisingly, it's used to provide a sour flavor in foods. Charred onion—the heat tames the bite and brings out some sweetness—and a little honey provide a modestly sweet ballast for the tart sumac. A dry cast-iron pan is perfect for charring the onion.

CHARRED ONION AND SUMAC VINAIGRETTE

MAKES ABOUT ½ CUP [120 ML]

One 1-in- [2.5-cm-] thick slice yellow onion

1 Tbsp sherry vinegar

2 tsp honey or light agave nectar

¾ tsp ground sumac

1 medium garlic clove, germ removed (see page 13), grated or minced to a paste

Kosher salt

Freshly ground black pepper

⅓ cup [80 ml] mild-flavored extra-virgin olive oil

In a small cast-iron or nonstick skillet over medium heat, place the onion slice and cook, undisturbed, until charred, about 15 minutes, flipping it once halfway through. Remove the onion to a cutting board, let cool briefly, and then mince.

In a glass jar, combine the vinegar, honey, sumac, garlic, ½ tsp salt, and ¼ tsp pepper and swirl to dissolve the salt. Add the minced onion and olive oil, screw on the lid tightly, and shake until the ingredients are well combined. Let stand to allow the flavors to meld, about 15 minutes. Taste and adjust the seasoning with additional salt and pepper, if necessary. Shake to recombine the vinaigrette just before using.

EXTRAS

Cucumbers, celery, grilled or roasted bell peppers, grape or cherry tomatoes, avocado, peaches, mango, fresh mint, fresh flat-leaf parsley, fresh dill, chickpeas, bulgur, Israeli couscous, lentils, toasted pistachios or walnuts, feta cheese, grilled Halloumi cheese

SERVE ON:

- **Romaine**
- **Green leaf lettuce**
- **Shredded cabbage**
- **Spinach**
- **Baby kale**
- **Lacinato kale**
- **Artichoke hearts**
- **Sliced tomatoes**
- **Summer squash**
- **Roasted cauliflower**
- **Roasted root vegetables (beets, carrots, parsnips, turnips)**
- **Grilled or roasted fennel**
- **Roasted sweet potatoes**
- **Roasted winter squash**
- **Seared duck breast**
- **Grilled or roasted lamb**

PINOT NOIR
VINAIGRETTE

A bit of reduced red wine gives this vinaigrette bold fruit flavor, complexity, and a suave presence. At the risk of dating ourselves, we think of it as the Ricardo Montalbán of vinaigrettes. Pinot Noir is our first choice for this vinaigrette because of its light to medium body and notes of plum and cherry, but any fruity red wine without oakiness or excessive tannins will work well. Back in our days as editors at Cook's Illustrated, we learned that reducing red wine slowly, rather than at a boil, helps preserve its flavor; hence, the medium heat we use to reduce it here.

MAKES ⅔ CUP [160 ML]

¾ cup [180 ml] Pinot Noir or other dry, fruity, non-oakey, light- to medium-bodied red wine

1 Tbsp red wine vinegar

2 Tbsp minced shallot

2 tsp honey or light agave nectar

Kosher salt

Freshly ground black pepper

⅓ cup [80 ml] extra-virgin olive oil

In a medium skillet over medium-high heat, bring the wine and vinegar to a brisk simmer. Turn the heat to medium and simmer until the mixture is reduced to about ¼ cup [60 ml], about 5 minutes. Pour into a glass jar and let cool completely.

Add the shallot, honey, ½ tsp salt, and ⅛ tsp pepper to the jar and swirl to dissolve the salt. Add the olive oil, screw on the lid tightly, and shake until the ingredients are well combined. Let stand to allow the flavors to meld, about 15 minutes. Taste and adjust the seasoning with additional salt and pepper, if necessary. Shake to recombine just before using.

SERVE ON:

- Any type of lettuce or salad greens
- Roasted beets
- Roasted carrots
- Cooked cabbage
- Grilled or seared salmon
- Grilled steak
- Grilled or roasted lamb
- Seared duck breast
- Chicken livers

EXTRAS

Grilled or roasted onions, grilled or roasted fennel, roasted or sautéed mushrooms, grilled peaches, figs, pears, plums, dried cherries, toasted walnuts, fresh flat-leaf parsley, fresh goat cheese, blue cheese, Parmigiano-Reggiano cheese, cooked crumbled bacon or pancetta

LEMON-PARMESAN VINAIGRETTE

With ingredients that are few but bold—salty, nutty, Parmigiano-Reggiano; tart lemon; and pungent garlic—this vinaigrette may be simple but it means business. We were first introduced to it on a kale salad that has earned pride of place in our permanent salad rotation.

MAKES ABOUT ⅔ CUP [160 ML]

2½ Tbsp fresh lemon juice

1 small garlic clove, germ removed (see page 13), grated or minced to a paste

Kosher salt

Freshly ground black pepper

⅓ cup [80 ml] extra-virgin olive oil

2 Tbsp finely grated Parmigiano-Reggiano cheese

In a glass jar, combine the lemon juice, garlic, ½ tsp salt, and ½ tsp pepper and swirl to dissolve the salt. Add the olive oil and Parmigiano-Reggiano, screw on the lid tightly, and shake until the ingredients are well combined. Let stand to allow the flavors to meld, about 15 minutes. Taste and adjust the seasoning with additional salt and pepper, if necessary. Shake to recombine just before using.

EXTRAS

Sautéed or steamed snow peas, grape or cherry tomatoes, roasted bell peppers, roasted or sautéed mushrooms, fresh basil, fresh flat-leaf parsley, toasted pine nuts, farro, Israeli couscous, olives, fried capers, anchovies, hard-cooked eggs

SERVE ON:

Romaine

Green leaf lettuce

Butter lettuce

Spinach

Baby kale

Lacinato kale

Summer squash

Roasted asparagus

Roasted or steamed broccoli or Broccolini

Roasted cauliflower

Braised leeks

Roasted Brussels sprouts

Grilled or roasted onions or fennel

Steamed or roasted baby artichokes

Roasted potatoes

SOUTHEAST ASIAN-STYLE LIME DRESSING

This dressing contains the basic flavors of som tam, or Thai green papaya salad. It's a feisty, high-impact mixture, but surprisingly, it works with a variety of foods—fruits such as mango and pineapple (and green papaya, of course), vegetables such as grilled eggplant and shredded cabbage, and proteins such as shrimp and tofu. We use a combination of light brown sugar and granulated sugar—brown sugar echoes the caramel-y notes of palm sugar that's used in traditional Thai papaya salad, and the granulated sugar prevents the dressing from becoming too dark in color. If you like, you can use all brown or all granulated sugar. No oil is used here.

SERVE ON:

- **Romaine**
- **Red or green leaf lettuce**
- **Shredded cabbage**
- **Mango**
- **Pineapple**
- **Pomelo segments**
- **Grilled eggplant**
- **Roasted or steamed broccoli or Broccolini**
- **Grilled steak, chicken, or pork**
- **Grilled or poached shrimp or squid**
- **Fried tofu**

MAKES ABOUT ½ CUP [120 ML]

1 small garlic clove, germ removed (see page 13)

1 or 2 Thai chiles, seeded

Pinch of kosher salt

¼ cup [60 ml] fresh lime juice

3½ Tbsp fish sauce

2 Tbsp packed light brown sugar

1½ Tbsp granulated sugar

Using a chef's knife, chop the garlic and push it to one side of the cutting board. Chop the chile(s), and then add the garlic. Sprinkle the mixture with the salt and continue to chop, occasionally mashing the mixture with the flat of the knife blade, until very finely minced and almost puréed.

In a small bowl, combine the lime juice, fish sauce, brown sugar, granulated sugar, and garlic-chile mixture and stir until the sugars dissolve. Let stand to allow the flavors to meld, about 15 minutes. Stir to recombine before using.

EXTRAS

Cucumber, red onion, red bell pepper, grape or cherry tomatoes, fresh cilantro, fresh mint, green onions, roasted peanuts, toasted unsweetened coconut, fried shallots

Packed with umami and all-star powers of emulsification, miso is a fantastic ingredient for salad dressings with a Japanese flavor profile. There are many different varieties of miso—here we use white, or shiro, which has a mild flavor and a touch of natural sweetness. In this dressing, the meaty flavor of miso meets a little heat from fresh ginger and freshness from orange juice and zest.

The variation of this dressing is sweet, spicy, salty, and umami-rich: the combination of fresh ginger and Sriracha creates a complex piquancy that will keep you coming back for more.

MISO DRESSING WITH GINGER AND ORANGE

MAKES ABOUT ½ CUP [120 ML]

3 Tbsp white (shiro) miso

2 Tbsp rice vinegar

2 Tbsp neutral oil, such as safflower, sunflower, or canola

1½ tsp grated peeled fresh ginger

1 tsp light agave nectar

1 tsp toasted sesame oil

⅛ tsp finely grated orange zest, plus 1½ Tbsp fresh orange juice

Kosher salt

Freshly ground white pepper

In a small bowl, combine the miso, vinegar, neutral oil, ginger, agave nectar, sesame oil, orange zest, orange juice, a pinch of salt, and a pinch of pepper and whisk until the dressing is smooth and uniform. Let stand to allow the flavors to meld, about 15 minutes. Taste and adjust the seasoning with additional salt and pepper, if necessary. Briskly stir to recombine just before using.

EXTRAS

Radishes, carrots, cucumbers, grape or cherry tomatoes, thinly sliced sweet onions, grilled or roasted onions, green onions, Asian pear, orange, toasted sesame seeds

FIERY MISO DRESSING

Substitute 1½ tsp Sriracha for the orange zest and proceed as directed.

SERVE ON:

Romaine

Red or green leaf lettuce

Butter lettuce

Spinach

Shredded cabbage

Roasted or steamed asparagus

Roasted or steamed green beans, broccoli, or Broccolini

Grilled eggplant

Roasted beets

Roasted carrots

Grilled or seared salmon

Grilled chicken

WAFU
DRESSING

This basic, easy-to-make, Japanese-style dressing features nuttiness from sesame seeds and sesame oil, subtle pungency from grated onion, and umami notes from soy sauce. (In case you're wondering, wafu translates to "Japanese-style.") If you want some extra spark and complexity, add a little grated fresh ginger or Japanese mustard (called karashi).

SERVE ON:

Romaine

Red or green leaf lettuce

Mesclun

Mizuna

Spinach

Watercress

Shredded cabbage

Steamed green beans

Grilled eggplant

Summer squash

Grilled or seared salmon or meaty white fish

MAKES ABOUT ⅔ CUP [160 ML]

¼ cup [60 ml] rice vinegar

3 Tbsp soy sauce

1 Tbsp sugar

¼ tsp freshly ground white pepper

2 Tbsp neutral oil, such as safflower, sunflower, or canola

1 tsp toasted sesame oil

2 tsp grated onion

1½ tsp sesame seeds, toasted

In a glass jar, combine the vinegar, soy sauce, sugar, and pepper and swirl to dissolve the sugar. Add the neutral oil, sesame oil, onion, and sesame seeds; screw on the lid tightly; and shake until the ingredients are well combined. Let stand to allow the flavors to meld, about 15 minutes. Shake to recombine just before using.

EXTRAS

Grape or cherry tomatoes, cucumber, radishes, roasted or steamed asparagus, sautéed or steamed snow peas, shelled edamame, Asian pear, green onions, *wakame* (a type of seaweed), toasted sesame seeds

KALE SALAD WITH PINE NUTS, PROSCIUTTO CRISPS, AND LEMON-PARMESAN VINAIGRETTE

SERVES 3 AS A LIGHT MAIN COURSE OR 4 AS A SALAD COURSE OR SIDE DISH

Timid palates beware: With minerally, lightly bitter kale; a brassy, garlicky dressing; salty, porky prosciutto crisps; and resinous pine nuts, this salad is a gathering of bold, raucous, but terrifically delicious, flavors. Rubbing the dressing into the kale and allowing it to stand for about 30 minutes softens the leaves so they have a more pleasing texture, and it also gives the flavors a chance to meld. We implore you NOT to skip this step.

¼ cup [30 g] pine nuts

8 oz [230 g] Lacinato kale, stemmed and torn into bite-size pieces

3 Tbsp Lemon-Parmesan Vinaigrette (page 59), plus more as needed

Kosher salt

Freshly ground black pepper (optional)

2 to 3 Tbsp finely grated Parmigiano-Reggiano cheese

3 or 4 pieces Prosciutto Crisps (page 106), broken into rough ½-in [12-mm] bits

In a small skillet over medium heat, toast the pine nuts, stirring frequently, until fragrant and golden, about 5 minutes. Transfer to a small plate and let cool completely.

Put the kale in a large bowl and drizzle in the viniagrette. With your hands, mix the kale, rubbing the dressing into the leaves and making sure that every piece is coated. Let stand at room temperature until the kale softens slightly, about 30 minutes.

Toss the kale to recombine, and taste a piece. If you like, drizzle with more vinaigrette, sprinkle with salt and pepper, if using, and toss again.

Transfer the kale to a serving bowl or divide among individual plates. Sprinkle with the pine nuts, Parmigiano-Reggiano, and prosciutto crisps. Serve immediately.

GRILLED STEAK AND RADICCHIO SALAD WITH ASIAN PEAR AND PINOT NOIR VINAIGRETTE

SERVES 4 AS A MAIN COURSE

With its supple grain and beefy flavor, skirt steak is our cut of choice here. It has a long, narrow shape, so feel free to cut it in half, or even in thirds, so that it's easier to handle on the grill. If skirt steak isn't available, flank steak also works well. It'll take a little longer to cook, though, because it's thicker. Be sure to use a neutral oil, such as sunflower, safflower, or canola, for oiling the grill grate.

This dish is adapted from a recipe by Barton Seaver, who suggests sprinkling on a little grated nutmeg. It's an unusual salad seasoning, but goes nicely with the Pinot Noir Vinaigrette.

½ cup [45 g] very thinly sliced red onion

1¼ lb [570 g] beef skirt steak

Kosher salt

Freshly ground black pepper

2 small heads radicchio, cored and torn into roughly 2-in [5-cm] pieces

2 cups [25 g] lightly packed flat-leaf parsley leaves, torn if large

1 large Asian pear, quartered, cored, and thinly sliced

1 recipe Pinot Noir Vinaigrette (page 58)

Freshly grated nutmeg (optional)

In a small bowl, cover the onion slices with cold water and let soak for 15 minutes. Drain, pat dry with paper towels, and set aside.

Prepare a hot fire in a charcoal grill or preheat a gas grill on high for 15 minutes. Generously season the skirt steak with salt and pepper. Clean and oil the grill grate and grill the steak (covered, if using a gas grill) until well-seared and medium-rare, 4 to 6 minutes, turning once halfway through grilling; the cooking time will depend on the thickness of the meat. Transfer the steak to a cutting board, cover loosely with foil, and let rest for 10 minutes. Very thinly cut the steak into slices on the diagonal against the grain.

In a large bowl, combine the radicchio, parsley, most of the onion, most of the Asian pear, about half of the vinaigrette, ½ tsp salt, and ½ tsp pepper and toss until well combined. Taste and adjust the seasoning with additional salt and pepper, if necessary. Arrange in a bed on a large serving platter. Dust sparingly with grated nutmeg (if using).

Arrange the sliced steak over the salad, sprinkle lightly with salt and pepper, and drizzle with the remaining vinaigrette. Top with the remaining onion and Asian pear. Serve immediately.

SPINACH, DELICATA SQUASH, AND APPLE SALAD WITH
MAPLE-MUSTARD VINAIGRETTE

SERVES 4 AS A LIGHT MAIN COURSE

With an oblong shape, creamy yellow color, and variegated orange and green striations, Delicata squash is in season from late summer through the fall. We like it for its creamy texture and lightly sweet flavor—and also because the skin is edible, so prep is a breeze. To get some real browning on at least one side of the squash slices, we don't turn them over while they roast.

¼ cup [40 g] chopped pecans or walnuts

2 medium Delicata squash, scrubbed, ends trimmed, halved lengthwise, seeded, and cut into ¾-in [2-cm] half-moon slices

1 Tbsp extra-virgin olive oil

Kosher salt

Freshly ground black pepper

⅔ cup [90 g] very thinly sliced red onion

6 cups [120 g] loosely packed fresh baby spinach

1 recipe Maple-Mustard Vinaigrette (page 49)

½ medium crisp apple (such as Gala, Fuji, or Braeburn), peeled, cored, and cut into matchsticks

⅓ cup [45 g] sweetened dried cranberries

Adjust an oven rack to the center position and preheat the oven to 425°F [220°C]. Line a large rimmed baking sheet with aluminum foil.

In a small skillet over medium heat, toast the pecans, stirring frequently, until fragrant and golden, about 5 minutes. Transfer to a small plate and let cool completely.

In a medium bowl, toss the squash slices with the olive oil and ½ tsp salt and season with pepper. Distribute the squash in a single layer on the prepared baking sheet and roast without turning until just tender, 20 to 25 minutes. Let cool to room temperature on the baking sheet.

Meanwhile, in a small bowl, cover the onion slices with cold water and let soak for about 15 minutes. Drain, pat dry with paper towels, and set aside.

In a large bowl, toss the spinach with half of the vinaigrette until coated. Taste and adjust the seasoning with salt and pepper, if necessary. Arrange the spinach in a bed on a large serving platter. Arrange the squash slices on the spinach and drizzle evenly with half the remaining dressing. Add the onion, apple, and remaining dressing to the large bowl, toss to coat, and scatter evenly over the squash. Sprinkle the toasted pecans and the cranberries over the salad. Serve immediately.

RICH

Cooking bacon slowly over medium heat helps ensure that the fat renders thoroughly and that drippings form in the skillet—and both are key to the flavor of this vinaigrette. We use only the bacon fat in the dressing, so you're left with bacon bits to sprinkle on the salad—or to gobble down when no one is looking. This vinaigrette is best when slightly warm; all the salad ingredients it dresses should be at room temperature.

BACON—
BLACK PEPPER
VINAIGRETTE

MAKES ABOUT ½ CUP [120 ML]

4 slices bacon, chopped

2 Tbsp minced shallot

2 Tbsp apple cider vinegar, preferably raw unfiltered

1 Tbsp packed brown sugar

1 tsp Dijon mustard

½ tsp freshly ground black pepper

Kosher salt

2½ Tbsp mild-flavored extra-virgin olive oil

Set a fine-mesh strainer over a small heatproof bowl. Line a small plate with a double layer of paper towels.

In a medium skillet over medium heat, fry the bacon, stirring occasionally, until crisp, the fat is rendered, and drippings have formed in the pan, about 12 minutes. Pour the contents of the skillet into the prepared strainer, and shake the strainer to encourage as much fat as possible to drain into the bowl. Set aside the bacon fat. Pour the bacon bits onto the prepared plate and set aside.

Add the shallots to the skillet, turn the heat to medium-low, and cook, stirring constantly, until softened and fragrant, 1 to 2 minutes. Turn off the heat, add the vinegar, and, using a wooden spoon, scrape up the browned bits from the bottom of the pan. Pour the vinegar mixture into a heatproof jar or bowl, add the brown sugar, mustard, pepper, and ½ tsp salt, and swirl to dissolve the sugar and salt.

Add 2 Tbsp of the reserved bacon fat and the olive oil to the warm mixture in the jar, screw on the lid tightly, and shake until the ingredients are well combined. Taste and adjust the seasoning with additional salt, if necessary. Shake and use immediately.

EXTRAS **Roasted or sautéed mushrooms, pears, peaches, nectarines, dates, toasted nuts (hazelnuts, pecans, almonds), farro, barley, wild rice, lentils, aged Cheddar or Gouda cheese, hard-cooked eggs**

SERVE ON:

Romaine

Spinach

Escarole

Frisée

Grilled radicchio

Baby or Lacinato kale

Cooked cabbage

Roasted or grilled asparagus

Roasted broccoli or Broccolini, cauliflower, or winter squash

Roasted root vegetables (beets, carrots, celery root, parsnips, potatoes, sweet potatoes, turnips)

Grilled or roasted onions

Grilled corn or eggplant

Grilled steak or pork

Grilled or seared salmon or scallops

BROWNED BUTTER
VINAIGRETTE

Butter in a vinaigrette? Yes! But not just any butter—fragrant and flavorful browned butter, which is butter that has been cooked until the milk solids (the bits that separate out to the bottom) turn toasty and chestnut in color and the mixture gives off an amazing nutty aroma. The transformation is nothing short of remarkable.

The small amount of oil in this rich dressing aids with emulsification and helps keep the dressing more fluid than it would be with just the butter. Still, the vinaigrette is best used warm, so put it on greens that can stand up to a bit of heat. It's also important to make sure that the leaves—or vegetables or fruits—in your salad are at room temperature.

SERVE ON:

- **Romaine**
- **Spinach**
- **Escarole**
- **Frisée**
- **Baby kale**
- **Grilled radicchio**
- **Cooked cabbage**
- **Roasted or grilled asparagus**
- **Roasted Brussels sprouts, cauliflower, broccoli, or Broccolini**
- **Roasted root vegetables (beets, carrots, celery root, parsnips, sweet potatoes, turnips)**
- **Roasted winter squash**
- **Grilled or seared scallops**

MAKES ABOUT ½ CUP [120 ML]

2 Tbsp sherry vinegar

1 tsp pure maple syrup

Kosher salt

Freshly ground black pepper

4 Tbsp [55 g] unsalted butter

1½ Tbsp neutral oil, such as sunflower or canola

In a glass jar, combine the vinegar, maple syrup, ½ tsp salt, and ¼ tsp pepper, swirl to dissolve the salt, and set aside.

In a small, heavy skillet or saucepan over medium-high heat, warm the butter until fully melted. Continue cooking, occasionally swirling the pan, until the milk solids at the bottom begin to take on a little color, 4 to 5 minutes. Continue to cook, stirring and scraping the bottom of the pan with a silicone spatula to ensure even browning, until the butter smells toasty and nutty and the milk solids are deeply browned—about the color of dark maple syrup. Immediately pour the butter into a small bowl, whisk in the oil, and let cool until just warm to the touch.

Add the butter mixture to the jar with the vinegar mixture, screw on the lid tightly, and shake until the ingredients are well combined. Taste and adjust the seasoning with additional salt and pepper, if necessary. Shake to recombine and use immediately.

EXTRAS

Roasted or sautéed mushrooms, radishes, apples, pears, apricots, pitted sweet cherries, figs, pomegranate arils, dried fruit, dates, toasted nuts (walnuts, hazelnuts, pecans, almonds, pistachios), cooked peeled chestnuts, farro, barley, wild rice

Avocado ranch dressing has been around for a while, but our version tastes especially fresh and vibrant because we forgo the usual mayonnaise and sour cream. For optimal flavor and texture, make sure your avocado is fully ripe. Surprisingly, even though this dressing contains quick-to-discolor avocado, it keeps for a couple of days (with plastic wrap pressed to the surface), though after that the color and flavors begin to dull.

AVOCADO RANCH DRESSING

MAKES ABOUT ⅔ CUP [160 ML]

½ ripe, medium Hass avocado, pitted

Kosher salt

Freshly ground black pepper

¼ cup [60 ml] buttermilk

1 Tbsp neutral oil, such as safflower, sunflower, canola, or avocado

1 Tbsp fresh lemon juice, plus more as needed

1 small garlic clove, germ removed (see page 13), grated or minced to a paste

2 tsp minced fresh flat-leaf parsley

2 tsp minced fresh chives

Using a knife, score the flesh of the avocado in a crosshatch pattern, cutting all the way down to, but not through, the skin. Scoop the flesh into a shallow medium bowl. Add ½ tsp salt and ¼ tsp pepper and use a rubber spatula or the back of the spoon to mash the avocado until it's smooth, with only a few tiny lumps.

Add the buttermilk, oil, lemon juice, and garlic to the avocado and whisk until the dressing is smooth and uniform. Add the parsley and chives and stir to incorporate them. Let stand to allow the flavors to meld, about 15 minutes. Taste and adjust the seasoning with additional salt and pepper, if necessary. Adjust the consistency with up to 1 tsp of water, if necessary, before using.

EXTRAS

Cherry or grape tomatoes, bell peppers, cucumbers, radishes, thinly sliced red onion, roasted green chiles, grilled corn, cooked crumbled bacon, freshly ground black pepper

SERVE ON:

Romaine

Iceberg

Green leaf lettuce

Escarole

Sliced tomatoes

Summer squash

Fried green tomatoes

Grilled or fried chicken cutlets, crab cakes or fish cakes

Grilled or seared shrimp

Roasted potatoes

SOURDOUGH
CAESAR
DRESSING

Romaine

Iceberg

Green leaf lettuce

Escarole

Grilled radicchio

Spinach

Roasted broccoli, Broccolini, or cauliflower

Artichoke hearts

Roasted or steamed asparagus

Steamed green beans

Sliced tomatoes

Summer squash

Grilled or roasted onions

Roasted winter squash

Grilled chicken

Our editor, Sarah Billingsley, turned us on to the notion of using bread to thicken a salad dressing. Here, in this unconventional Caesar dressing, we use sourdough in place of egg to create a creamy consistency. The bread also contributes flavor, so it's worth seeking out a good-quality loaf.

Parmigiano-Reggiano cheese, though not an ingredient in traditional Caesar dressing, shows up in many recipes and is undeniably simpatico with the other flavors, so we've included it. Anchovy is traditional, and if you like its fishy flavor, by all means, double the quantity. When you blend the sourdough and liquid to break down the bread, the mixture will splatter, so cover the beaker with a kitchen towel.

This recipe presents the perfect opportunity to employ the Garlic Rub (see page 23).

MAKES ABOUT ½ CUP [120 ML]

¼ cup [10 g] crustless ½-in [12-mm] cubes of sourdough bread

1 Tbsp fresh lemon juice

¾ tsp Worcestershire sauce

2 Tbsp water

1 large oil-packed anchovy fillet

1 medium garlic clove, germ removed (see page 13), grated or minced to a paste

½ tsp Dijon mustard

2 Tbsp finely grated Parmigiano-Reggiano cheese

⅓ cup [80 ml] extra-virgin olive oil

Kosher salt

Freshly ground black pepper

In the beaker of an immersion blender, combine the bread, lemon juice, Worcestershire, and water. Purée until the bread is broken down into mushy crumbs, about 15 seconds. Let the bread mixture stand for about 10 minutes to soften.

Add the anchovy, garlic, mustard, Parmigiano-Reggiano, olive oil, ¼ tsp salt, and ¼ tsp pepper to the beaker. Purée until the mixture is thick and smooth, about 15 seconds. Let stand to allow the flavors to meld, about 15 minutes. Taste and adjust the seasoning with additional salt and pepper, if necessary. Briskly stir to recombine just before using. (If the dressing is thicker than you like, whisk in 1 to 2 tsp more water to thin it.)

EXTRAS **Cherry tomatoes, cucumbers, celery, fresh or roasted fennel, sautéed or roasted mushrooms, fresh basil or parsley, salami or mortadella, marinated white anchovies, Parmigiano-Reggiano or fresh mozzarella cheese, hard-cooked eggs**

TAHINI, LEMON, AND HARISSA DRESSING

There are hot sauces, and then there's harissa. With roots in Morocco and Tunisia, brick-red harissa is aromatic and complex, with rich layers of flavor from chiles (which can be dried, fresh, or a combination), garlic, olive oil, coriander, cumin, and caraway. You can make harissa at home but prepared versions are available in cans, tubes, and jars in the international aisle of well-stocked markets and in Middle Eastern specialty stores. Brands of store-bought harissa vary in spiciness—start with 1 Tbsp and add more if you want a punchier dressing. Bright lemon and earthy tahini are natural matches for harissa.

MAKES ABOUT ½ CUP [120 ML]

3 Tbsp extra-virgin olive oil

2 Tbsp tahini

1 Tbsp harissa

½ tsp finely grated lemon zest,
plus 1½ Tbsp fresh lemon juice

1 large garlic clove, germ removed (see page 13),
grated or minced to a paste

Kosher salt

Freshly ground black pepper

2 Tbsp water

In the beaker of an immersion blender, combine the olive oil, tahini, harissa, lemon zest, lemon juice, garlic, ¾ tsp salt, ¼ tsp pepper, and water. Purée until the mixture is smooth. Let stand to allow the flavors to meld, about 15 minutes. Taste and adjust the seasoning with salt and pepper, if necessary. Stir to recombine just before using.

EXTRAS

Cucumbers, carrots, grape or cherry tomatoes, celery, radishes, sweet bell peppers, sweet onion, pomegranate arils, fresh cilantro, toasted sesame seeds, toasted nuts (pine nuts or pistachios), chickpeas, Israeli couscous, olives

SERVE ON:

Romaine

Green leaf lettuce

Spinach

Roasted beets or carrots

Steamed green beans

Roasted broccoli, Broccolini, cauliflower, winter squash, or sweet potatoes

Grilled or roasted onions or eggplant

Grilled or roasted chicken

Grilled meaty white fish

JAPANESE-STYLE TOASTED SESAME DRESSING

This nubby-textured dressing/sauce is modeled after Japanese gomae, which translates as "sesame sauce"—a preparation that's used to dress various vegetables, most commonly spinach. When shopping, look for unhulled sesame seeds, which are a bit larger and plumper than tiny, flat, hulled sesame seeds and have more flavor intensity. Unhulled sesame seeds are often found in the bulk section of natural foods stores, and Asian markets are likely to sell toasted unhulled sesame in flip-top plastic shakers. These toasted seeds simplify prep because they can be used straight from the container. But if you suspect the store's turnover to be slow, we say take a pass and toast your own. If only hulled sesame seeds are available, stir ¼ tsp toasted sesame oil into the dressing.

SERVE ON:

- Romaine
- Green leaf lettuce
- Shredded cabbage
- Baby kale
- Endive
- Blanched and well-dried spinach, kale, or Swiss chard
- Roasted or steamed asparagus, broccoli, or Broccolini
- Steamed green beans
- Grilled or seared salmon or tuna
- Grilled pork tenderloin

MAKES ABOUT ½ CUP [120 ML]

6 Tbsp [60 g] unhulled sesame seeds

2½ Tbsp soy sauce

1 Tbsp light agave nectar

1 Tbsp mirin (Japanese sweet rice wine)

2 tsp sake

1 tsp rice vinegar

¼ tsp freshly ground white pepper

In a medium skillet over medium heat, toast the sesame seeds, stirring frequently, until fragrant and golden, 6 to 8 minutes. Transfer to a plate and let cool completely.

In a small bowl, whisk together the soy sauce, agave nectar, mirin, sake, rice vinegar, and pepper. Set aside.

Transfer the sesame seeds to a spice grinder or the beaker of an immersion blender. Pulse until the seeds are finely ground and powdery, but not pasty; do not overprocess.

Add the ground sesame to the soy sauce mixture and whisk to combine before using; the dressing will be rather thick. (If the dressing is thicker than you like, whisk in 1 to 2 tsp water to thin it.)

EXTRAS

Grape or cherry tomatoes, cucumber, radishes, fennel, sautéed or steamed snow peas, roasted or sautéed mushrooms, Asian pears, plums, oranges, green onions

SWEET AND SPICY
PEANUT
DRESSING

This recipe turns to Asia for inspiration, but it doesn't actually board the plane. As in any dressing, the idea here is to balance the flavors. So as not to eclipse the peanut butter, we don't go wild with either the sweet (brown sugar) or the hot (Sriracha), but you can add a little extra hot, if you like. Mild rice vinegar works well with the brown sugar, but we add a tiny bit of fresh lime juice for extra lift.

MAKES ABOUT ½ CUP [120 ML]

**3 Tbsp neutral oil, such as
safflower, sunflower, or canola**

2 Tbsp salted natural-style smooth peanut butter

1 Tbsp rice vinegar

1 Tbsp packed dark or light brown sugar

1¼ tsp Sriracha, or to taste

1 tsp soy sauce

½ tsp fresh lime juice

**1 large garlic clove, germ removed (see page 13),
grated or minced to a paste**

Freshly ground black pepper

2 Tbsp water

In the beaker of an immersion blender, combine the oil, peanut butter, vinegar, brown sugar, Sriracha, soy sauce, lime juice, garlic, ½ tsp pepper, and water. Purée until the mixture is smooth. Let stand to allow the flavors to meld, about 15 minutes. Taste for seasoning and add more pepper and Sriracha, if necessary. Stir to recombine the dressing just before using.

EXTRAS

Grape or cherry tomatoes, carrots, thinly sliced sweet onion, bell peppers, sliced jalapeños, Peppadew peppers, fresh cilantro, green onions, fried shallots

SERVE ON:

Romaine

Iceberg

Green leaf lettuce

Shredded cabbage

Cucumber

Grilled or roasted eggplant

Steamed green beans

Roasted or steamed broccoli or Broccolini

Roasted sweet potatoes

Sliced tomatoes

Summer squash

Blanched and well-dried spinach or Swiss chard

Grilled chicken

Fried tofu

LEMON-
TOASTED ALMOND
DRESSING
WITH ALEPPO PEPPER

Made from a variety of chile pepper that's native to southern Turkey, near the Syrian city of Aleppo, dried Aleppo chile flakes have a bright flavor, subtle fruitiness, notes of mint (and many say cumin), and a mild heat that quickly dissipates on the palate. You can order the spice online or purchase it in brick-and-mortar specialty shops. Otherwise, substituting sweet paprika and a pinch of cayenne pepper is your best bet. This dressing is creamy and rich, thanks to the almonds puréed into the mixture. To get the best flavor out of the almonds, make sure to toast them until they're dark golden brown and very aromatic.

SERVE ON:

- Romaine
- Green leaf lettuce
- Escarole
- Grilled radicchio
- Braised leeks
- Roasted or steamed broccoli or Broccolini
- Roasted cauliflower or winter squash
- Roasted root vegetables (beets, carrots, celery root, parsnips, turnips)
- Grilled eggplant
- Summer squash
- Sliced tomatoes
- Artichoke hearts
- Grilled shrimp or squid
- Grilled or seared salmon or other meaty fish

MAKES ABOUT ⅔ CUP [160 ML]

1 Tbsp slivered almonds

2 Tbsp fresh lemon juice

Kosher salt

Freshly ground black pepper

1½ Tbsp water

1½ tsp honey

1 small garlic clove, germ removed (see page 13), chopped

½ tsp Aleppo chile flakes

⅓ cup [80 ml] extra-virgin olive oil

In a small skillet over medium heat, toast the almonds, stirring frequently, until deeply browned and richly fragrant, 8 to 10 minutes. Transfer to a small plate and let cool completely.

In the beaker of an immersion blender, combine the toasted almonds, lemon juice, ½ tsp salt, ⅛ tsp black pepper, and water. Let stand to allow the almonds to soften slightly, about 10 minutes.

Add the honey, garlic, Aleppo chile flakes, and olive oil to the beaker and purée until the dressing is smooth and has the consistency of drinkable yogurt. Let stand to allow the flavors to meld, about 15 minutes. Taste and adjust seasoning with additional salt and black pepper, if necessary. Briskly stir to recombine just before using.

EXTRAS

Cucumber, grape or cherry tomatoes, thinly sliced sweet onion, fennel, bell peppers, roasted red peppers, radishes, kohlrabi, fresh cilantro, fresh flat-leaf parsley, farro, chickpeas, toasted sliced almonds

BUTTERMILK BLACK-AND- BLUE DRESSING

This dressing packs a big, twofold punch because there's no mayo or sour cream interfering with the deliciously funky blue cheese, and a generous dose of black pepper plays up the blue's piquancy. Choose a blue cheese with an assertive flavor and a firm yet creamy texture—Roquefort, for example. Gorgonzola dolce would be too mild and soft, and Cabrales would be too strong and dry.

MAKES ABOUT ½ CUP [120 ML]

6 Tbsp [55 g] blue cheese, crumbled, at room temperature

⅓ cup [80 ml] buttermilk, at room temperature, plus up to 1 Tbsp

1 small garlic clove, germ removed (see page 13), grated or minced to a paste

½ tsp freshly ground black pepper

⅛ tsp sugar

1 Tbsp minced fresh chives

1¼ tsp white wine vinegar, plus more as needed

Kosher salt (optional)

In a medium bowl, combine the blue cheese, buttermilk, garlic, pepper, and sugar. Use a rubber spatula or dinner fork to mash the mixture until it's smooth and uniform, with only a few tiny lumps. Stir in the chives and vinegar. Let stand to allow the flavors to meld, about 15 minutes. Taste and adjust the seasoning with salt, if necessary, and additional vinegar, and adjust the consistency with up to 1 Tbsp buttermilk, if necessary. Briskly stir to recombine just before using.

EXTRAS

Cherry or grape tomatoes, thinly sliced sweet onion, bell peppers, fennel, radishes, blanched sugar snap peas, figs, pears, avocado, toasted walnuts, chopped smoked almonds, crumbled cooked bacon

SERVE ON:

Romaine (try grilled romaine wedges!)

Iceberg

Green leaf lettuce

Roasted broccoli, Broccolini, beets, or cauliflower

Grilled or roasted onions

Summer squash

Sliced tomatoes

Fried green tomatoes

Burgers

ROASTED GARLIC
DRESSING

Roasting garlic transforms the pungency and bite to a nutty sweet-ness and softens the cloves so they're creamy and spreadable. In this versatile dressing, roasted garlic also acts as an emulsifying agent, giving it a rich, full-bodied consistency.

MAKES ABOUT ½ CUP [120 ML]

1 medium head garlic, outermost papery skin removed

6 Tbsp [90 ml] extra-virgin olive oil

1 Tbsp sherry vinegar

2 tsp fresh lemon juice

½ tsp minced fresh thyme

Kosher salt

Freshly ground black pepper

2 Tbsp minced fresh flat-leaf parsley

Adjust an oven rack to the center position and preheat the oven to 400°F [200°C].

Slice off the top third of the garlic head to expose the tops of the cloves and set on a sheet of aluminum foil. Drizzle the garlic with 1 Tbsp of the olive oil, draw up the foil and fold the edges to create a packet, and roast until fragrant and the cloves are soft, about 30 minutes. Open the foil and continue roasting until the cut surfaces of the cloves are golden brown, about 10 minutes longer. Let cool to room temperature.

Squeeze the garlic cloves out of their skins onto a cutting board. Roughly mash with a fork.

In the beaker of an immersion blender, combine the roasted garlic, vinegar, lemon juice, thyme, ½ tsp salt, ¼ tsp pepper, and the remaining 5 Tbsp [75 ml] olive oil. Purée until the mixture is smooth. Let stand to allow the flavors to meld, about 15 minutes. Taste and adjust the seasoning with additional salt and pepper, if necessary. Add the parsley and stir briskly to recombine just before using.

Artichoke hearts, cucumbers, celery, cherry or grape tomatoes, sweet bell peppers, raw or roasted bell peppers, roasted green chiles, marinated cherry peppers, pickled beets, fennel, radishes, sweet onions, grilled or roasted asparagus, grilled corn, grilled or roasted eggplant, sautéed or roasted mushrooms, avocado, figs, grapes, fresh basil, fresh dill, olives, capers, white beans, chickpeas, lentils, farro, barley, bulgur, Israeli couscous, quinoa, oil-packed tuna, fresh mozzarella cheese, feta cheese, Parmigiano-Reggiano cheese, cooked crumbled bacon, Spanish-style chorizo, hard-cooked eggs

COUNTRY-STYLE GREEK SALAD WITH PITA CRISPS AND ROASTED GARLIC DRESSING

SERVES 4 AS A LIGHT MAIN COURSE OR 6 AS A SIDE DISH

This salad is something of a mash-up of chunky lettuce-less Greek salad called horiatiki ("village style") and the classic Middle Eastern salad with pita called fattoush. (Don't think we didn't consider calling this something goofy like "horiatoush" or "fatiki.") In lieu of the red wine and lemon juice vinaigrette that's standard for Greek salad, we've opted for our Roasted Garlic Dressing (after all, we claim that it's good on just about anything!). That said, an equal quantity of Charred Onion and Sumac Vinaigrette (page 57) also works nicely.

¼ **medium red onion, sliced into ⅛-in [4-mm] quarter moons**

1 lb [455 g] **cherry tomatoes, halved if small or medium, quartered if large**

1 medium **cucumber, peeled, halved, seeded, and sliced ⅛ in [4 mm] thick**

⅔ cup [95 g] **pitted Kalamata olives, halved**

¾ cup [9 g] **fresh mint leaves, torn**

3 Tbsp **chopped fresh dill**

½ recipe **Seasoned Pita Crisps (page 96), broken into roughly ¾-in [2-cm] pieces**

1 recipe **Roasted Garlic Dressing (page 86)**

Kosher salt

Freshly ground black pepper

1 cup [140 g] **feta cheese, crumbled**

In a medium bowl, cover the onion slices with cold water and let soak for 15 minutes. Drain and pat dry with paper towels.

In a large bowl, combine the onion slices, tomatoes, cucumber, olives, mint, and dill and toss just until combined. Add the pita crisps and toss just once or twice. Drizzle the dressing over the salad, sprinkle with ¼ tsp salt and ½ tsp pepper, and toss just until combined. Sprinkle the feta over the salad and gently toss once or twice, until the feta is just incorporated. (Do not overmix or the cheese will break down and make the salad murky.) Taste and adjust the seasoning with salt, pepper, and more dressing, if necessary.

Transfer the salad to a serving bowl or platter and serve immediately.

ROASTED CARROT, BROCCOLINI, AND CHICKEN SALAD WITH
TAHINI, LEMON, AND HARISSA DRESSING

SERVES 4 AS A MAIN COURSE

This hearty salad—and several others in this book—demonstrates our fondness for mixing roasted and fresh ingredients. Here, the roasted carrots contribute a concentrated earthy sweetness, Broccolini provides green, mineral notes, and the romaine delivers refreshing, watery crunch. The nutty, tangy, spicy dressing buoys and unifies the roasted and fresh components. If your Broccolini stems are thick, you may want to peel them. Honestly, though, we rarely bother.

1 lb [455 g] carrots, peeled and cut into even 2-in-by-½-in [5-cm-by-12-mm] sticks

2 Tbsp extra-virgin olive oil

Kosher salt

Freshly ground black pepper

8 oz [230 g] Broccolini, trimmed and cut into 2-in [5-cm] pieces

8 cups [255 g] loosely packed torn romaine leaves

4 medium green onions, trimmed, whites thinly sliced and greens sliced on the bias into 1-in [2.5-cm] lengths

1 recipe Tahini, Lemon, and Harissa Dressing (page 79)

2 cups [200 g] shredded rotisserie chicken

Adjust an oven rack to the center position and preheat the oven to 400°F [200°C]. Line a rimmed baking sheet with aluminum foil.

In a large bowl, toss the carrots with 1 Tbsp of the olive oil and ¼ tsp salt and season with pepper. Spread the carrots in a single layer on the prepared baking sheet, cover tightly with foil, and roast for 10 minutes.

Meanwhile, in the same bowl, toss the Broccolini with the remaining 1 Tbsp olive oil and ¼ tsp salt and season with pepper. Uncover the roasted carrots, toss, and arrange them over half the baking sheet. Add the Broccolini to the empty half of the sheet (do not cover) and roast until the carrots are browned and tender and the Broccolini is tender, 10 to 15 minutes. Let cool to room temperature.

In the same bowl, combine the romaine, green onion green parts, and about half the dressing; season with salt and pepper and toss to coat well. Taste and adjust the seasoning with additional salt and pepper, if necessary, and spread on a serving platter to form a bed for the carrot mixture.

In the same bowl, toss the roasted carrots, Broccolini, chicken, and most of the green onion white parts with the remaining dressing to coat. Arrange the carrot mixture over the salad, sprinkle with the remaining green onion white parts and serve immediately.

ARUGULA, PLUM, AND FENNEL SALAD WITH
JAPANESE-STYLE TOASTED SESAME DRESSING

SERVES 4 TO 6 AS A SALAD COURSE OR SIDE DISH

This simple salad of just four components, plus dressing, is elegant and unusual. To get the right balance of sweet, savory, tart, and peppery, make sure that the plums are juicy and ripe—prepare the salad in the summertime when stone fruits are in season. It's best to assemble the dish in the kitchen but toss it at the table because it's prettier in the "before" state, and also because arugula wilts very quickly. The dressing is highly seasoned, so we find it's not necessary to add extra salt and pepper during tossing. But do pass additional dressing at the table for those who might want a little more.

6 cups [120 g] loosely packed baby arugula

½ medium fennel bulb, trimmed, halved, cored, and cut crosswise into ⅛-in [4-mm] slices

2 medium green onions, dark and light green parts, thinly sliced on the bias

2 ripe medium red or black plums, halved, pitted, and cut into ⅜-in [1-cm] wedges

3 Tbsp Japanese-Style Toasted Sesame Dressing (page 80), plus more for serving

In a large bowl, toss together the arugula, fennel, and green onions and transfer to a serving platter. Scatter the plum slices over the greens and top with small spoonfuls of the dressing.

Just before serving, gently toss the salad to coat with the dressing. Pass additional dressing at the table.

RUSTIC CROUTONS

Walk into a party carrying a bag of crisp, craggy croutons rather than the usual chips, and people may wonder about you. Until they try one, that is, and learn first hand that the old potato chip adage "I bet you can't eat just one" applies to your croutons, too.

Fresh bread makes great croutons; lightly stale bread gives them a more resilient crunch, but don't overdo it by using really stale bread. Choose a hearty white loaf with a dense, chewy crumb. Beyond that, use whatever type appeals to you—French, Italian, country white, peasant, or sourdough are just a few of the possibilities. Keep a close eye on the croutons as they bake—the timing varies with different types of bread and how dry each bread may be. Croutons are best when fresh. Don't worry about storage time—they won't last long enough for it to be an issue.

MAKES ABOUT 6 CUPS [210 G]

12 oz [340 g] hearty French, Italian, country white, peasant, or sourdough bread, crusts trimmed, and bread torn into roughly 1-in [2.5-cm] pieces

3 Tbsp extra-virgin olive oil

Kosher salt

Adjust an oven rack to the center position and preheat the oven to 350°F [180°C].

In a large bowl, toss the bread, olive oil, and ½ tsp salt until all the bread is lightly coated with oil. On a baking sheet, spread the bread in an even layer. Bake, stirring every 5 minutes, until the pieces are deep golden brown, 15 to 20 minutes. Let cool completely on the baking sheet. The croutons will crisp up as they cool.

SERVE ON:

Any type of greens except delicate ones

Soups

Eat them by the handful!

SEASONED PITA CRISPS

Whereas Rustic Croutons (page 95) satisfy with a brawny crunch and a hint of chew, pita crisps press our buttons with their svelte form and light crispness. They're pretty great seasoned simply with olive oil and salt, but that's just a starting point for whatever dried herbs strike your fancy. Lots of recipes instruct you to separate the two rounds of each pita, which we dutifully did until deciding that (1) it was a nuisance, and (2) we rather liked the double crunch of the intact pitas, so now we don't bother with it. We do, however, brush the pitas with oil and season them while they're whole, which promotes more even coverage than the usual routine of tossing the cut pita wedges in a bowl with the oil. Plain and whole-wheat pita work equally well.

SERVE ON:

- **Any type of greens except delicate ones**
- **Chopped salads**
- **Soups**
- **With dips**

MAKES 30 CRISPS

3 pitas, about 8 in [20 cm] in diameter
2 to 3 Tbsp extra-virgin olive oil
Kosher salt
Freshly ground black pepper
1 to 2 tsp dried herbs or herb mixture of choice

Adjust an oven rack to the center position and preheat the oven to 350°F [180°C].

Brush both sides of each pita with olive oil, and sprinkle lightly with salt, pepper, and the herbs, crumbling the herbs as you sprinkle. Cut each pita into ten wedges, arrange them in a single layer on a baking sheet, and bake until the crisps are deep golden brown, 16 to 18 minutes, turning them over halfway through the baking time. Let cool completely on the baking sheet. The pita will crisp up with cooling.

These are best served the day they're made.

There are two good reasons to make this recipe: You'll have fried shallots that are perfectly crisp and so delicious that you'll want to eat them out of hand, and you'll have shallot oil to use as a flavoring in salad dressings, as a garnish on soups, and as a seasoning in countless other dishes. Shallot oil can overwhelm subtle flavors, so use it judiciously.

The best vessel for frying shallots is a wok, because its shape allows you to use a minimal amount of oil and makes for easy stirring. If you don't have a wok, use a smallish saucepan that's quite narrow but has some depth.

FRIED SHALLOTS

MAKES ABOUT 1¼ CUPS [60 G] FRIED SHALLOTS AND ABOUT ½ CUP [120 ML] SHALLOT OIL

⅔ cup [160 ml] neutral oil, such as canola, safflower, or sunflower, plus more as needed

8 oz [230 g] shallots, sliced into very thin rings

Big pinch of kosher salt

SERVE ON:

- **Salads with Southeast Asian flavors**
- **Leafy salads**
- **Grain salads**
- **Sandwiches**
- **Soups**
- **Stir-fries**
- **Fried rice**

Set a large fine-mesh strainer over a heatproof bowl. Line a plate with a double-thick layer of paper towels.

In a wok or a small, narrow saucepan over medium heat, warm the oil. When it just begins to shimmer, add a shallot slice—it should sizzle gently. If it doesn't, allow the oil to heat for an additional 1 to 2 minutes and test again. When the oil is ready, add all the shallots, turn the heat to medium-high, and stir well. (It's fine if the shallots are not fully submerged in oil because they will shrink as they fry. However, if they are standing well above the surface of the oil, pour in an additional 2 to 3 Tbsp oil.) Fry the shallots, stirring frequently and adjusting the heat as needed to maintain a gentle but steady bubbling action, until they just begin to turn light golden, about 10 minutes. Turn the heat to medium and fry, stirring constantly because the shallots will now color quickly, until they smell toasty and are medium brown (the shallots will continue to cook with residual heat to a shade darker), 1 to 2 minutes longer.

Immediately pour the shallots and oil into the prepared strainer. Carefully shake the strainer or stir the shallots to drain as much oil as possible. Distribute the shallots on the prepared plate. Sprinkle with the salt and let cool completely.

Fried shallots will keep in an airtight container at room temperature for about 1 week. Shallot oil will keep in a well-sealed jar in the refrigerator for up to 1 month.

FRICO

(A.K.A. PARMESAN WAFERS)

SERVE ON:

Any type of greens

Slightly chewy at the center and crisp around the edges, these Italian cheese wafers are super simple to make. Make sure not to cook them past a pale gold color. At that stage they'll taste of toasted cheese, but if they overcook they'll take on a bitter note. A nonstick or very well-seasoned cast-iron skillet is essential for making them, as is good-quality cheese. Beyond garnishing salads, frico make a terrific savory nibble with cocktails, antipasto platter element, or cracker stand-in alongside a steaming bowl of soup or stew.

MAKES EIGHT TO TEN 3-IN [7.5-CM] WAFERS

½ tsp olive oil

1⅓ cups [115 g] Parmigiano-Reggiano or aged Asiago cheese, grated on the large holes of a box grater

Line a baking sheet with paper towels.

Brush the olive oil over the bottom of a large, heavy nonstick skillet and set over medium heat. For each wafer, place 2 Tbsp of the grated cheese in 2½-in [6-cm] rounds in the skillet, leaving about 2 in [5 cm] between the rounds. (Depending on the size of the skillet, it should accommodate four or five rounds. Make in as many batches as necessary.) Cook the cheese, undisturbed, until it melts, bubbles, spreads slightly, and begins to brown very lightly around the edges, about 3 minutes. With a thin, heatproof spatula, carefully loosen and flip the wafers; cook the other side, undisturbed, until very pale gold, about 1 minute longer. (If the pan appears to overheat or smoke, adjust the heat accordingly.) Transfer the frico from the pan to the prepared baking sheet and repeat with the remaining cheese (additional oil will not be necessary after the initial batch). Let cool to room temperature.

Frico are best served within 3 hours of cooking.

THYME-SCENTED ROASTED CHICKPEAS

SERVE ON:

Any type of greens except delicate ones

The flavors of these chickpeas are reminiscent of socca, a crisp chickpea-flour pancake seasoned with extra-virgin olive oil and black pepper that's a popular street food in and around old Nice, on the Riviera. And without actual plane tickets, we'll take any Riviera reminder we can get! These are a decidedly snackable salad topping.

MAKES ABOUT 1 CUP [120 G]

One 15-oz [425-g] can chickpeas, drained, rinsed, and dried with paper towels

2 tsp extra-virgin olive oil

½ tsp ground cumin

Kosher salt

Freshly ground black pepper

1½ tsp minced fresh thyme

Adjust an oven rack to the center position and preheat the oven to 450°F [230°C].

In a medium bowl, combine the chickpeas, 1 tsp of the olive oil, the cumin, and ¾ tsp salt; season with pepper and toss until evenly coated. Spread the chickpeas in a single layer on a small, rimmed baking sheet and roast, stirring every 10 minutes, until shrunken, browned, and crisp, about 40 minutes.

Immediately return the hot chickpeas to the bowl, add the remaining 1 tsp olive oil and the thyme, and toss to distribute. Return the chickpeas to the baking sheet and let cool to room temperature.

Store in an airtight container at room temperature for up to 1 week.

Sweet and salty spiced nuts are a terrific salad garnish—one that adds layers of flavor and great texture. Walnuts and/or pecans are primary here because their crevices are perfect for trapping the sugar-spice coating; almonds and/or cashews are also included because they add interesting shapes and flavors. Chopping the nuts before cooking means they'll be ready for sprinkling on a salad as soon as they have cooled; but if you plan on eating these out of hand, you could leave the nuts whole (they may take a couple minutes longer to toast).

SPICED NUTS

MAKES 2 CUPS [280 G]

1½ cups [180 g] very coarsely chopped walnuts or pecans, or a combination

½ cup [60 g] slivered almonds or coarsely chopped cashews, or a combination

3 Tbsp sugar

¾ tsp chili powder

¾ tsp kosher salt

¼ tsp freshly ground black pepper

⅛ tsp ground allspice

⅛ tsp cayenne pepper (optional)

1½ Tbsp unsalted butter

1 Tbsp water

SERVE ON:

Any type of greens except delicate ones

Slaw

Roasted or grilled vegetables

Ice cream (if you dare)

Line a rimmed baking sheet with parchment paper.

In a large nonstick skillet over medium-low heat, toast the nuts, stirring frequently, until deep golden and very fragrant, 10 to 12 minutes. Transfer the nuts to the prepared baking sheet. Wipe out but do not wash the skillet.

In a large bowl, stir together 1½ Tbsp of the sugar, the chili powder, salt, black pepper, allspice, and cayenne (if using).

Set the skillet over medium heat and add the remaining 1½ Tbsp sugar, the butter, and the water. Cook the mixture, stirring to combine, until bubbling and slightly thickened, 1 to 2 minutes. Add the nuts, stir to coat, and cook until sticky and glazed and the moisture has evaporated, about 2 minutes. Immediately pour the nuts into the sugar-spice mixture and toss until evenly coated. Return the nuts to the baking sheet and let cool completely.

Store in an airtight container at room temperature for up to 1 week.

SAVORY GRANOLA

In this recipe, crunchy, toasty granola gets savory notes from thyme, Worcestershire, black pepper, and garlic powder but also has a subtle sweetness from a bit of brown sugar. Make sure to keep this granola separate from the regular stuff to prevent any breakfast-time surprises.

SERVE ON:

- Any type of greens except delicate ones
- Roasted vegetables
- Cooked cabbage

MAKES ABOUT 3¼ CUPS [300 G]

1 cup [100 g] old-fashioned rolled oats

⅓ cup [40 g] chopped walnuts

⅓ cup [40 g] slivered almonds

¼ cup [35 g] raw pepitas (shelled pumpkin seeds)

1 Tbsp sesame seeds

1 Tbsp millet

3 Tbsp extra-virgin olive oil

1 egg white

2½ Tbsp packed light brown sugar

1 tsp minced fresh thyme

1 tsp kosher salt

½ tsp freshly ground black pepper

½ tsp Worcestershire sauce

½ tsp smoked paprika

⅛ tsp cayenne pepper (optional)

⅛ tsp garlic powder

Adjust an oven rack to the center position and preheat the oven to 325°F [165°C]. Line a rimmed baking sheet with parchment paper.

In a medium bowl, combine the oats, walnuts, almonds, pepitas, sesame seeds, and millet and stir until well mixed.

In a small bowl, whisk together the olive oil, egg white, brown sugar, thyme, salt, black pepper, Worcestershire, paprika, cayenne (if using), and garlic powder until homogenous.

Pour the liquid mixture over the oat mixture and stir with a rubber spatula until everything is evenly moistened. Empty the mixture onto the center of the prepared baking sheet and, using the spatula, firmly pat the mound into an even layer about ¼ in [6 mm] thick. (Don't worry about the shape that the layer forms.)

Bake until the granola is golden brown at the center and a little darker around the edges, about 25 minutes. Use a thin metal spatula to scrape up the granola, allowing it to break into large shards. Flip the shards as best you can with the spatula, but don't break them into small bits. Distribute in an even layer and continue to bake until the granola is very deep golden brown, 10 to 15 minutes longer. Let cool completely on the baking sheet. The granola will crisp up as it cools. Break the granola into ½-in [12-mm] pieces, or smaller if you prefer.

Store in an airtight container at room temperature for up to 2 weeks.

Resist the temptation to use thick-cut bacon—regular bacon absorbs the glaze better. Make sure to use a rimmed baking sheet so it will confine the fat rendered from the bacon. And while you're at it, don't forget to line the sheet with aluminum foil or parchment paper or cleanup will be a nightmare. The aroma of glazed bacon cooking in the oven may bring marauders to the kitchen, and with them their tendencies for bacon thievery while your back is turned. Forewarned is forearmed.

GLAZED BACON

MAKES 10 SLICES

10 slices bacon

2½ Tbsp packed light brown sugar

1½ Tbsp fresh orange juice

SERVE ON:

Any type of greens except delicate ones

Cooked cabbage

Adjust an oven rack to the center position and preheat the oven to 375°F [190°C]. Line a rimmed baking sheet with aluminum foil or parchment paper and set a large wire rack in the prepared sheet.

Arrange the bacon slices in a single layer on the wire rack. Roast the bacon until the slices render some of their fat and shrink significantly, about 10 minutes.

Meanwhile, in a small bowl, whisk together the brown sugar and orange juice (the sugar may not fully dissolve).

Carefully remove the baking sheet from the oven and use a heat-proof brush to lightly dab the bacon with about half the brown sugar mixture. Continue roasting until the brown sugar mixture adheres to the bacon and appears glossy, about 8 minutes. Carefully remove the baking sheet from oven and flip the slices. Lightly dab with the remaining brown sugar mixture and continue roasting until the brown sugar mixture is glazed and glossy, about 8 minutes longer. Carefully transfer the slices to a plate, let cool, and then chop or crumble, if desired.

Store in an airtight container at room temperature for up to 1 day.

PROSCIUTTO
CRISPS

SERVE ON:

▶ **Any type of greens**

Baking prosciutto slices intensifies their flavor, making them super-porky and salty, as well as delicately and irresistibly crisp. Prosciutto crisps can be used whole, broken into shards, or crumbled into bits, depending on the application. They're a perfect garnish on many types of salads, as well as on baked potatoes and scrambled eggs. For making crisps, buy presliced packaged prosciutto. The slices are uniformly thin and are separated by layers of paper or plastic, so they can be peeled apart easily. If you have the prosciutto sliced to order at the deli counter, you may bring home a skein that's impossible to separate into slices.

MAKES 6 TO 8 PIECES

6 to 8 very thin prosciutto slices

Adjust an oven rack to the center position and preheat the oven to 350°F [180°C]. Line a baking sheet with parchment paper.

Lay as many prosciutto slices as will fit in a single layer on the prepared baking sheet. If necessary, bake in batches or use a second parchment paper–lined baking sheet. Bake until the prosciutto slices are shrunken and slightly darkened, about 15 minutes, carefully flipping each slice halfway through. Transfer the slices to a wire rack and let cool completely. The prosciutto will crisp up with cooling.

Store in an airtight container at room temperature for up to 1 day.

INDEX OF HEARTY SERVE-ONS

INDEX